ORDNANCE SURVEY

Cycle TOURS

24 one-day routes in

Avon, Somerset & Wiltshire

Compiled by Nick Cotton

HAMLYN

Contents

4 *Key to routes*
6 *Quick reference chart*
8 *Avon, Somerset and Wiltshire*
9 *Abbreviations and instructions*
10 *Fact boxes*
Page diagrams
11 *Before you go*
12 *Cross-profile diagrams*
13 *Tips for touring*
15 *Transporting your bike*
16 *Legend to 1:50 000 maps*

On-road routes

18 **1** *From Thornbury to Berkeley in the Severn Vale*
24 **2** *Easy Cotswold riding west of Malmesbury*
30 **3** *Easy Cotswold riding east of Malmesbury*
36 **4** *From Clevedon to Clifton*
42 **5** *Bath to Castle Combe and Lacock*
48 **6** *River valleys and canals near Marlborough*
54 **7** *High on the Mendips*
60 **8** *The Somerset Levels south of Wedmore*
66 **9** *The roof of Exmoor, west of Dulverton*
72 **10** *Over the Brendon Hills, east of Dulverton*
78 **11** *From the Somerset Levels to the Blackdown Hills west of Ilminster*
84 **12** *From the hills to the Levels northeast of Ilminster*
90 **13** *Valleys and downland west of Wilton*
96 **14** *A circle around Salisbury via Alderbury, Porton and the Woodfords*

Off-road routes

102 **1** *Steep Cotswold hills between Bristol and Bath*

106 **2** *Ancient earthworks around Avebury*

110 **3** *Over Dundry Hill and along little-known tracks southwest of Bristol*

114 **4** *A slice of Cheddar and a taste of the Mendips*

118 **5** *The Mendips north of Wells*

122 **6** *High ridges between three Exmoor villages*

126 **7** *Around Wimbleball Lake, Exmoor*

130 **8** *Chalk ridges north of Mere*

134 **9** *Ancient roads in Wiltshire*

138 **10** *Ridge tracks and ox droves west of Wilton*

Acknowledgements
Nick Cotton *back cover, 79, 85, 119, 131* • Pitkin Pictorials Limited *60-61, 134* • South West Water PLC *127* • Judy Todd *18, 25, 30, 48, 67, 73, 97, 107, 115, 123*

Back cover photograph: Swallowcliffe Down, north of Alvediston

First published by

Ordnance Survey
Romsey Road
Maybush
Southampton
SO16 4GU

and

Hamlyn, an imprint of
Reed Books
Michelin House
81 Fulham Road
London SW3 6RB

Second edition 1995
First impression 1995

A catalogue record for this atlas is available from the British Library

ISBN 0 600 58664 2
(Ordnance Survey ISBN 0 319 00767 7)

Made, printed and published in Great Britain

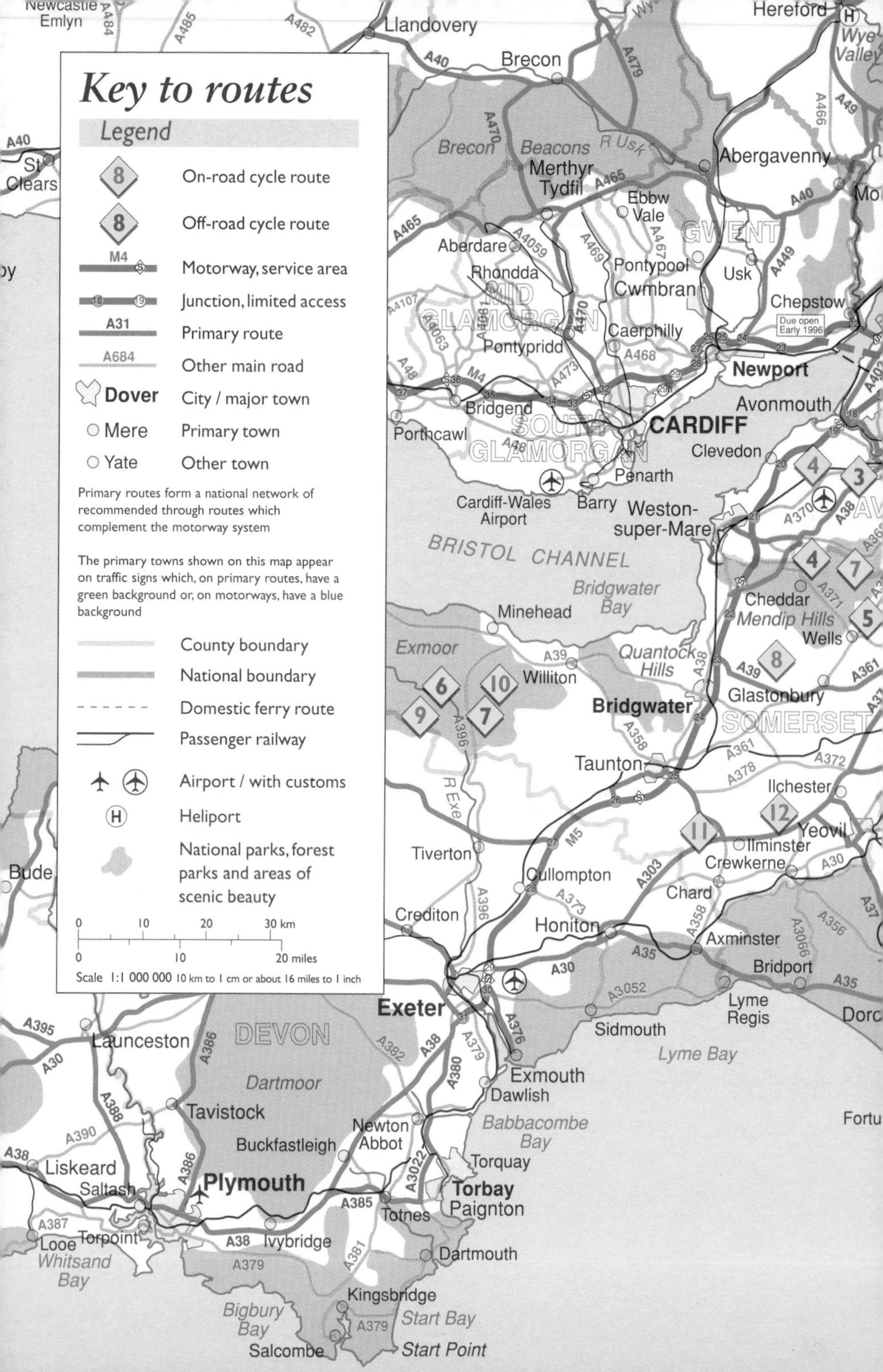
Key to routes
Legend
8 On-road cycle route
8 Off-road cycle route
M4 Motorway, service area
18 19 Junction, limited access
A31 Primary route
A684 Other main road
Dover City / major town
Mere Primary town
Yate Other town
Primary routes form a national network of recommended through routes which complement the motorway system
The primary towns shown on this map appear on traffic signs which, on primary routes, have a green background or, on motorways, have a blue background
County boundary
National boundary
Domestic ferry route
Passenger railway
Airport / with customs
Heliport
National parks, forest parks and areas of scenic beauty
0 10 20 30 km
0 10 20 miles
Scale 1:1 000 000 10 km to 1 cm or about 16 miles to 1 inch
Newcastle Emlyn
Llandovery
Hereford
Wye Valley
Brecon
Brecon Beacons
R Usk
Abergavenny
Merthyr Tydfil
Ebbw Vale
St Clears
GWENT
Aberdare
Rhondda
Pontypool
Cwmbran
Usk
Chepstow
Due open Early 1996
MID GLAMORGAN
Pontypridd
Caerphilly
Newport
Bridgend
Porthcawl
CARDIFF
Avonmouth
SOUTH GLAMORGAN
Clevedon
Penarth
Cardiff-Wales Airport
Barry
Weston-super-Mare
BRISTOL CHANNEL
Bridgwater Bay
Minehead
Cheddar
Mendip Hills
Wells
Exmoor
Quantock Hills
Williton
Glastonbury
Bridgwater
SOMERSET
Taunton
Ilchester
Yeovil
Ilminster
Tiverton
Crewkerne
Cullompton
Chard
Bude
Crediton
Honiton
Axminster
Bridport
Lyme Regis
Exeter
Sidmouth
DEVON
Launceston
Lyme Bay
Exmouth
Dartmoor
Dawlish
Tavistock
Babbacombe Bay
Newton Abbot
Buckfastleigh
Liskeard
Torquay
Plymouth
Saltash
Torbay
Paignton
Totnes
Looe
Torpoint
Ivybridge
Whitsand Bay
Dartmouth
Kingsbridge
Bigbury Bay
Start Bay
Salcombe
Start Point
R Exe

ENGLISH CHANNEL

Quick reference chart

	Route	Page	Distance (miles)	Grade (easy/moderate/ strenuous)	Links with other routes[1]	Tourist information centres[2]
	On-road routes					
1	*From Thornbury to Berkeley in the Severn Vale*	18	33			Bristol 0117-9260767
2	*Easy Cotswold riding west of Malmesbury*	24	28		3,5	Malmesbury 01666-823748
3	*Easy Cotswold riding east of Malmesbury*	30	29		2	Malmesbury 01666-823748
4	*From Clevedon to Clifton, west of Bristol*	36	32		7	Bristol 0117-9260767
5	*Bath to Castle Combe and Lacock*	42	35		2	Bath 01225-462831
6	*River valleys and canals near Marlborough*	48	36			Marlborough 01672-513989
7	*High on the Mendips*	54	37		4,8	Cheddar 01934-744071
8	*The Somerset Levels south of Wedmore*	60	32		7	Glastonbury 01458-32954
9	*The roof of Exmoor, west of Dulverton*	66	32		10	Minehead 01643-702624
10	*Over the Brendon Hills, east of Dulverton*	72	34		9	Minehead 01643-702624
11	*From the Somerset Levels to the Blackdown Hills west of Ilminster*	78	32		12	Ilminster 01460-57294
12	*From the hills to the Levels northeast of Ilminster*	84	29		11	Ilminster 01460-57294
13	*Valleys and downland west of Wilton*	90	25		14	Salisbury 01722-334956
14	*A circle around Salisbury via Alderbury, Porton and the Woodfords*	96	39		13	Salisbury 01722-334956

Route	Page	Distance (miles)	Grade (easy/moderate/strenuous)	Links with other routes[1]	Tourist information centres[2]
Off-road routes					
1 *Steep Cotswold hills between Bristol and Bath*	102	11			Bath 01225-462831
2 *Ancient earthworks around Avebury*	106	19			Marlborough 01672-513989
3 *Over Dundry Hill and along little-known tracks southwest of Bristol*	110	17			Bristol 0117-9260767
4 *A slice of Cheddar and a taste of the Mendips*	114	18		5	Wells 01749-744071
5 *The Mendips north of Wells*	118	16		4	Wells 01749-72552
6 *High ridges between three Exmoor villages*	122	18			South Molton 017695-4122
7 *Around Wimbleball Lake, Exmoor*	126	7,10, 17	to		South Molton 017695-4122
8 *Chalk ridges north of Mere*	130	15			Mere 01747-860341
9 *Ancient roads in Wiltshire*	134	25		10	Salisbury 01722-334956
10 *Ridge tracks and ox droves west of Wilton*	138	25		9	Salisbury 01722-334956

[1] ***Links with other routes*** Use this information to create a more strenuous ride or if you are planning to do more than one ride in a day or on a weekend or over a few days. The rides do not necessarily join: there may be a distance of up to three miles between the closest points. Several rides are in pairs, sharing the same starting point, which may be a good place to base yourself for a weekend.

[2] ***Tourist Information Centres*** You can contact them for details about accommodation. If they cannot help, there are many books that recommend places to stay. If nothing is listed for the place where you want to stay, try phoning the post office or the pub in the village to see if they can suggest somewhere.

Avon, Somerset and Wiltshire

From the high moorland of Exmoor to the honey-coloured stone of the southern Cotswolds, from the chalk downland of Salisbury Plain and the Marlborough Downs to the flat Somerset Levels and the Severn Vale, the area covered by this guide boasts an impressive variety of landscape. As well as natural wonders, there are still visible signs of Britain's earliest people in the vast number of ancient earthworks, tumuli and stone circles, the most famous of which are at Avebury and Stonehenge. A few thousand years after Stonehenge was finished, a different sort of stone, oolitic limestone, or Cotswold stone, was extensively quarried to create the much photographed Cotswold villages and the splendour of Bath and parts of Bristol. Several rides that start within a short distance of these two principal cities of the County of Avon stay on the flat areas of the Severn Vale on the dark peat Somerset Levels surrounding the mystical centre of Glastonbury, which provide the easiest cycling in southern England. More strenuous and challenging rides climb the Mendips, south of Bristol.

In the southeast corner of the region, Wilton, just west of Salisbury, is the starting point for four rides, two off-road and two on-road. The road routes tend to follow the lovely valleys that radiate out from here to the north and west, while the off-road rides are on the ridges, at times following old Roman roads over the chalk downland, at times, old coaching routes of ox droves.

Further west, two rides start from Ilminster, one to explore the southern part of the Somerset Levels, the other to climb to 1,000 feet on the Blackdown Hills. You will find the most challenging rides on Exmoor, starting from the charming town of Dulverton. Hard climbs are rewarded with fabulous ridge rides on the very roof of Exmoor, with occasional views out over the Bristol Channel.

Abbreviations and instructions

Instructions are given as concisely as possible to make them easy to follow while you are cycling. Remember to read one or two instructions ahead so that you do not miss a turning. This is most likely to occur when you have to turn off a road on which you have been riding for a fairly long distance and these junctions are marked ***Easy to miss*** to warn you.

If there appears to be a contradiction between the instructions and what you actually see, always refer to the map. There are many reasons why over the course of a few years instructions will need updating as new roads are built and priorities and signposts change.

If giving instructions for road routes is at times difficult, doing so for off-road routes can often be almost impossible, particularly when the route passes through woodland. With few signposts and buildings by which to orientate yourself, more attention is paid to other features, such as gradient and surface. Most of these routes have been explored between late spring and early autumn and the countryside changes its appearance very dramatically in winter. If in doubt, consult your map and check your compass to see that you are heading in the right direction.

Where I have encountered mud I have mentioned it, but this may change not only from summer to winter but also from dry to wet weather at any time during the year. At times you may have to retrace your steps and find a road alternative.

Some routes have small sections that follow footpaths. The instructions will highlight these sections where you must get off and push your bike. You may only ride on bridleways and by-ways so be careful if you stray from the given routes.

Directions

L	left
LH	left-hand
RH	right-hand
SA	straight ahead or straight across
bear L or R	make less than a 90-degree (right-angle) turn at a fork in the road or track or at a sharp bend so that your course appears to be straight ahead; this is often written as *in effect SA*
sharp L or R turn	is more acute than 90 degrees
sharp R/L back on yourself	an almost U-turn
sharp LH/RH bend	a 90-degree bend
R then L or R	the second turning is visible then immediately L from the first
R then 1st L	the second turning may be some distance from the first; the distance may also be indicated: *R, then after 1 mile L*

Junctions

T-j	T-junction, a junction where you have to give way
X-roads	crossroads, a junction where you may or may not have to give way
offset X-roads	the four roads are not in the form of a perfect cross and you will have to turn left then right, or vice versa, to continue the route

Signs

'Placename 2'	words in quotation marks are those that appear on signposts; the numbers indicate distance in miles unless stated otherwise
NS	not signposted
trig point	a trigonometrical station

Instructions

An example of an easy instruction is:

4 *At the T-j at the end of Smith Road by the White Swan PH R on Brown Street 'Greentown 2, Redville 3'.*

There is more information in this instruction than you would normally need, but things do change: pubs may close down and signs may be replaced, removed or vandalized.

An example of a difficult instruction is:

8 *Shortly after the brow of the hill, soon after passing a telephone box on the right next L (NS).*

As you can see, there is no T-junction to halt you in your tracks, no signpost indicating where the left turn will take you, so you need to have your wits about you in order not to miss the turning.

Fact boxes

The introduction to each route includes a fact box giving useful information:

Start

This is the suggested start point coinciding with instruction 1 on the map. There is no reason why you should not start at another point if you prefer.

Distance and grade

The distance is, of course, that from the beginning to the end of the route. If you wish to shorten the ride, however, the maps enable you to do so.

The number of drinks bottles indicates the grade:

Easy

Moderate

Strenuous

Page diagrams

The on-road routes occupy four pages of mapping each. The page diagrams on the introductory pages show how the map pages have been laid out, how they overlap and if any inset maps have been used.

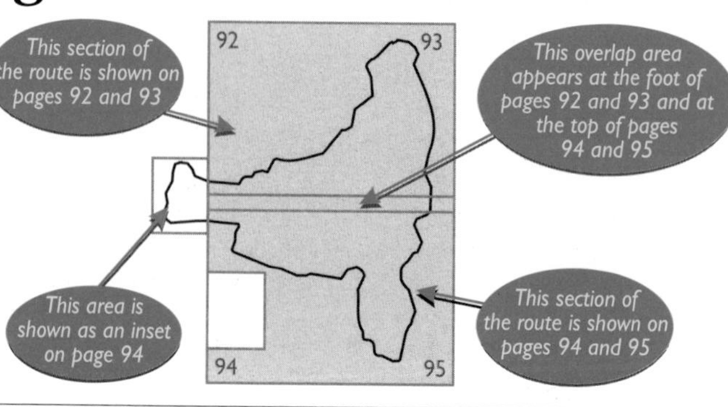

The grade is based on the amount of climbing involved and, for off-road rides, the roughness of the surface rather than the distance covered.

Remember that conditions may vary dramatically with the weather and seasons, especially along off-road routes

Terrain

This brief description of the terrain may be read in conjunction with the cross-profile diagram at the foot of the page to help you to plan your journey.

Nearest railway

This is the distance to the nearest station from the closest point on the route, not necessarily from the start. Before starting out you should check with British Rail for local restrictions regarding the carrying of bicycles.
(See page 15)

Refreshments

Pubs and teashops on or near the route are listed. The tankard symbols indicate pubs particularly liked by the author

Before you go

Preparing yourself

Fitness

- Cycling uses muscles in a different way from walking or running, so if you are beginning or returning to it after a long absence you will need time to train your muscles and become accustomed to sitting on a saddle for a few hours. Build up your fitness and stamina gradually and make sure you are using a bicycle that is the right size for you and suits your needs.

Equipment

- Attach the following items to the bike: bell, pump, light-brackets and lights, lock-holder and lock, rack and panniers or elastic straps for securing things to the rack, map holder. Unless it is the middle of summer and the weather is guaranteed to be fine, you will need to carry extra clothes, particularly a waterproof, with you, and it is well worth investing in a rack for this purpose.
- Wearing a small pouch around your waist is the easiest and safest way of carrying small tools and personal equipment. The basics are: Allen keys to fit the various Allen bolts on your bike, chainlink extractor, puncture repair kit, reversible screwdriver (slot and crosshead), small adjustable spanner, spare inner tube, tyre levers (not always necessary with mountain bike tyres), coins and a phonecard for food and telephone calls, compass.
- Additional tools for extended touring: bottom bracket extractor, cone spanners, freewheel extractor, headset spanners, lubricant, socket spanner for pedals, spare cables, spoke-key.

Clothing

- What you wear when you are cycling should be comfortable, allowing you, and most especially your legs, to move freely. It should also be practical, so that it will keep you warm and dry if and when the weather changes.
- **Feet** You can cycle in just about any sort of footwear, but bear in mind that the chain has oil on it, so do not use your very best shoes. Leather tennis shoes or something similar, with a smooth sole to slip into the pedal and toe clip are probably adequate until you buy specialist cycling shoes, which have stiffer soles and are sometimes designed for use with specialist pedals.
- **Legs** Cycling shorts or padded cycling underwear worn under everyday clothing make long rides much more comfortable. Avoid tight, non-stretch trousers, which are very uncomfortable for cycling and will sap your energy, as they restrict the movement of your legs; baggy tracksuit

bottoms, which can get caught in the chain and will sag around your ankles if they get wet. Almost anything else will do, though a pair of stretch leggings is probably best.

- ***Upper body*** What you wear should be long enough to cover your lower back when you are leaning forward and, ideally, should have zips or buttons that you can adjust to regulate your temperature. Several thin layers are better than one thick layer.
- ***Head*** A helmet may protect your head in a fall.
- ***Wet weather*** If you get soaked to your skin and you are tired, your body core temperature can drop very quickly when you are cycling. A waterproof, windproof top is essential if it looks like rain. A dustbin bag would be better than nothing but obviously a breathable waterproof material is best.
- ***Cold weather*** Your extremities suffer far more when you are cycling than when you are walking in similar conditions. A hat that covers your ears, a scarf around your neck, a pair of warm gloves and a thermal top and bottom combined with what you would normally wear cycling should cover almost all conditions.
- ***Night and poor light*** Wearing light-coloured clothes or reflective strips is almost as important as having lights on your bike. Reflective bands worn around the ankles are particularly effective in making you visible to motorists.

Preparing your bicycle

- You may not be a bicycle maintenance expert, but you should make sure that your bike is roadworthy before you begin a ride.
- If you are planning to ride in soft, off-road conditions, fit fat, knobbly tyres. If you are using the bike around town or on a road route, fit narrower, smoother tyres.
- Check the tyres for punctures or damage and repair or replace if necessary or if you are in any doubt. Keep tyres inflated hard (recommended pressures are on the side wall of the tyre) for mainly on-road riding. You do not need to inflate tyres as hard for off-road use; slightly softer tyres give some cushioning and get better traction in muddy conditions.
- Ensure that the brakes work efficiently. Replace worn cables and brake blocks.
- The bike should glide along silently. Tighten and adjust any part that is loose or rubbing against a moving part. Using a good-quality bike oil lubricate the hubs, bottom bracket, pedals where they join the cranks, chain and gear-changing mechanism from both sides. If the bike still makes grating noises, replace the bearings.
- Adjust the saddle properly. You can raise or lower it, move it forwards or backwards or tilt it up or down. The saddle height should ensure that your legs are working efficiently: too low and your knees will ache; too high and your hips will be rocking in order for your feet to reach the pedals.
- Some women find the average bike saddle uncomfortable because the female pelvis is a different shape from the male pelvis and needs a broader saddle for support. Some manufacturers make saddles especially for women.

Cross-profiles

The introduction to each route includes a cross-profile diagram. The vertical scale is the same on each diagram but the horizontal scale varies according to the length of the route

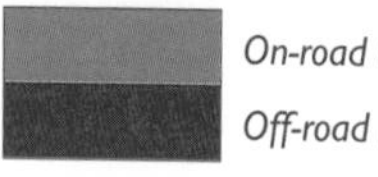

Tips for touring

The law

England and Wales have 120 000 miles of rights of way, but under the Wildlife and Countryside Act of 1968 you are allowed to cycle on only about 10 percent of them, namely on bridleways, by-ways open to all traffic (BOATS) and roads used as public paths (RUPPS).
The other 90 percent of rights of way are footpaths, where you may walk and usually push your bike, but not ride it. Local bylaws sometimes prohibit the pushing of bicycles along footpaths and although all the paths in this book have been checked, bylaws do sometimes change.

- You are not allowed to ride where there is no right of way. If you lose the route and find yourself in conflict with a landowner, stay calm and courteous, make a note of exactly where you are and then contact the Rights of Way Department of the local authority. It has copies of definitive maps and will take up the matter on your behalf if you are in the right.
- For further information on cycling and the law contact the Cyclists Touring Club (CTC) whose address can be found on the inside back cover.

Cycling techniques

If you are not used to cycling more than a few miles at a stretch, you may find initially that touring is tiring. There are ways of conserving your energy, however:

- Do not struggle in a difficult gear if you have an easier one. Let the gears help you up the hills. No matter how many gears a bike has, however, ultimately it is leg power that you need to get you up a hill. You may decide to get off and walk uphill with your bike to rest your muscles.
- You can save a lot of energy on the road by following close behind a stronger rider in his or her slipstream, but do not try this offroad. All the routes are circular, so you can start at any point and follow the instructions until you return to it. This is useful when there is a strong wind, as you can alter the route to go into the wind at the start of the ride, when you are fresh, and have the wind behind you on the return, when you are more tired.
- The main difference in technique between on-road and off-road cycling lies in getting your weight balanced correctly. When going down steep off-road sections, lower the saddle, keep the pedals level, stand up out of the saddle to let your legs absorb the bumps and keep your weight over the rear wheel. Control is paramount: keep your eyes on what lies ahead.

Steeple Hill
Grange Arch
Ridgeway Hill
Knowle Hill
Start / finish

Traffic

The rides in this book are designed to minimize time spent on busy roads, but you will inevitably encounter some traffic. The most effective way to avoid an accident with a motor vehicle is to be highly aware of what is going on around you and to ensure that other road users are aware of you.

- Ride confidently.
- Indicate clearly to other road users what you intend to do, particularly when turning right. Look behind you, wait for a gap in the traffic, indicate, then turn. If you have to turn right off a busy road or on a difficult bend, pull in and wait for a gap in the traffic or go past the turning to a point where you have a clear view of the traffic in both directions, then cross and return to the turning.
- Use your lights and wear reflective clothing at night and in poor light.
- Do not ride two-abreast if there is a vehicle behind you. Let it pass. If it cannot easily overtake you because the road is narrow, look for a passing place or a gate entrance and pull in to let it pass.

Maintenance

Mountain bikes are generally stronger than road bikes, but any bike can suffer. To prevent damage as far as possible:

- Watch out for holes and obstacles.
- Clean off mud and lubricate moving parts regularly.
- Replace worn parts, particularly brake blocks.

Riders also need maintenance:

- Eat before you get hungry, drink before you get thirsty. Dried fruit, nuts and chocolate take up little space and provide lots of energy.
- Carry a water bottle and keep it filled, especially on hot days. Tea, water and well-diluted soft drinks are the best thirst-quenchers.

Breakdowns

The most likely breakdown to occur is a puncture.

- Always carry a pump.
- Take a spare inner tube so that you can leave the puncture repair until later.
- Make sure you know how to remove a wheel. This may require an adjustable spanner or, in many cases, no tool at all, as many bikes now have wheels with quick-release skewers that can be loosened by hand.

Security

Where you park your bike, what you lock it with and what you lock it to are important in protecting it from being stolen.

- Buy the best lock you can afford.
- Lock your bike to something immovable in a well-lit public place.
- Locking two bikes together is better than locking them individually.
- Use a chain with a lock to secure the wheels and saddle to the frame. Keep a note of the frame number and other details, and insure, photograph and code the bike.

Lost and Found

The detailed instructions and the Ordnance Survey mapping in this book minimize the chances of getting lost. However, if you do lose your way:

- Ask someone for directions.
- Retrace the route back to the last point where you knew where you were.
- Use the map to rejoin the route at a point further ahead.

Transporting your bike

There are three ways of getting you and your bike to the start of a ride:

Cycle to the start or to a point along a route near your home.

Take the train. Always check in advance that you can take the bike on the train. Some trains allow only up to two bikes and you may need to make a reservation and pay a flat fee however long the journey. Always label your bike showing your name and destination station.

Travel by motor vehicle. You can carry the bikes:

- Inside the vehicle. With the advent of quick release mechanisms on both wheels and the seatpost, which allow a quick dismantling of the bike, it is possible to fit a bike in even quite small cars. It is unwise to stack one bike on top of another unless you have a thick blanket separating them to prevent scratching or worse damage. If you are standing them up in a van, make sure they are secured so they cannot slide around.
- On top of the vehicle. The advantages of this method are that the bikes are completely out of the way and are not resting against each other, you can get at the boot or hatch easily and the bikes do not obscure the number plate or rear lights and indicators. The disadvantages are that you use up more fuel, the car can feel uncomfortable in a crosswind and you have to be reasonably tall and strong to get the bikes on and off the roof.
- On a rack that attaches to the rear of the vehicle. The advantages are that the rack is easily and quickly assembled and disassembled, fuel consumption is better and anyone can lift the bikes on and off. The disadvantages are that you will need to invest in a separate board carrying the number plate and rear lights if they are obstructed by the bikes, you cannot easily get to the boot or hatch once the bikes have been loaded and secured, and the bikes are resting against each other so you must take care that they don't scrape off paint or damage delicate parts.
- Whichever way you carry the bikes on the outside of the vehicle, ensure that you regularly check that they are secure and that straps and fixings that hold them in place have not come loose. If you are leaving the bikes for any length of time, be sure they are secure against theft; if nothing else lock them to each other.

Code of Conduct

- Enjoy the countryside and respect its life and work
- Only ride where you know you have a legal right
- Always yield to horses and pedestrians
- Take all litter with you
- Don't get annoyed with anyone; it never solves any problems
- Guard against all risk of fire
- Fasten all gates
- Keep your dogs under close control
- Keep to public paths across farmland
- Use gates and stiles to cross fences, hedges and walls
- Avoid livestock, crops and machinery or, if not possible, keep contact to a minimum
- Help keep all water clean
- Protect wildlife, plants and trees
- Take special care on country roads
- Make no unnecessary noise

Legend to 1:50 000 maps

Roads and paths

Motorway

Service area S M 5 Elevated

Junction number 20

Motorway under construction

Trunk road

Unfenced Footbridge

A 46 (T)

Main road

Dual carriageway

A 420

Main road under construction

Secondary road

B 4348

Narrow road with passing places

A 855 B 885

Road generally more than 4 m wide

Bridge

Road generally less than 4 m wide

Other road, drive or track

Path

Gradient: 1 in 5 and steeper, 1 in 7 to 1 in 5

Gates Road tunnel

Passenger ferry Vehicle ferry

Ferry P Ferry V

Public rights of way (Not applicable to Scotland)

Footpath

Bridleway

Road used as a public footpath

Byway open to all traffic

Danger Area — Firing and test ranges in the area. Danger! Observe warning notices

Tourist information

Information centre, all year / seasonal

Parking

Picnic site

Viewpoint

Camp site

Caravan site

Youth hostel

Selected places of tourist interest

Public telephone

Motoring organisation telephone

Golf course or link

PC Public convenience (in rural areas)

Railways

Track: multiple or single

Track: narrow gauge

Bridges, footpath

Tunnel

Viaduct

Freight line, siding or tramway

Station, (a) principal, (b) closed to passengers

Level crossing (LC)

Embankment

Cutting

Rock features

Public rights of way indicated by these symbols have been derived from Definitive Maps as amended by the latest enactments or instruments held by Ordnance Survey and are shown subject to the limitations imposed by the scale of mapping. Further information may be obtained from the appropriate County or London Borough Council

The representation on this map of any other road, track or path is no evidence of the existence of a right of way

Water features

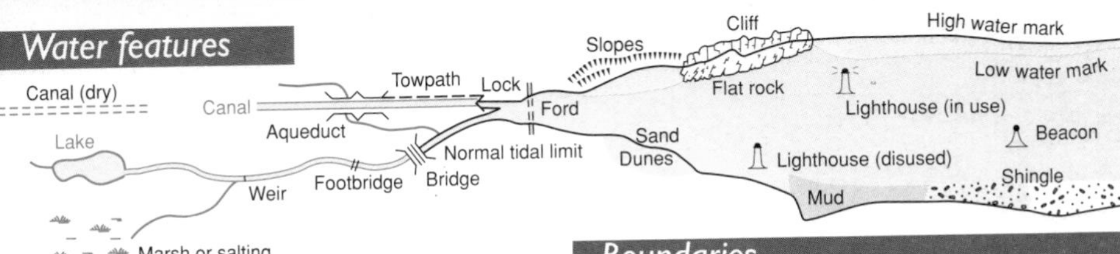

General features

Electricity transmission line (with pylons spaced conventionally)

Pipeline (arrow indicates direction of flow)

Buildings (ruin)

Public buildings (selected)

Bus or coach station

Coniferous wood

Non-coniferous wood

Mixed wood

Orchard

Park or ornamental grounds

Quarry

Spoil heap, refuse tip or dump

Radio or TV mast

Church or chapel with tower

Church or chapel with spire

Church or chapel without tower or spire

Chimney or tower

Glasshouse

Graticule intersection at 5' intervals

Heliport

Triangulation pillar

Windmill with or without sails

Windpump

Boundaries

National

London borough

National park or forest park

National Trust — NT open access; NT limited access

County, region or islands area

District

Abbreviations

P	Post office
PH	Public house
MS	Milestone
MP	Milepost
CH	Clubhouse
PC	Public convenience (in rural areas)
TH	Town hall, guildhall or equivalent
CG	Coastguard

Antiquities

VILLA	Roman
Castle	Non-Roman
⚔	Battlefield (with date)
☆	Tumulus
+	Position of antiquity which cannot be drawn to scale
𝔐	Ancient monuments and historic buildings in the care of the Secretaries of State for the Environment, for Scotland and for Wales and that are open to the public

Heights

50	Contours are at 10 metres vertical interval
·144	Heights are to the nearest metre above mean sea level

Heights shown close to a triangulation pillar refer to the station height at ground level and not necessarily to the summit

1 From Thornbury to Berkeley in the Severn Vale

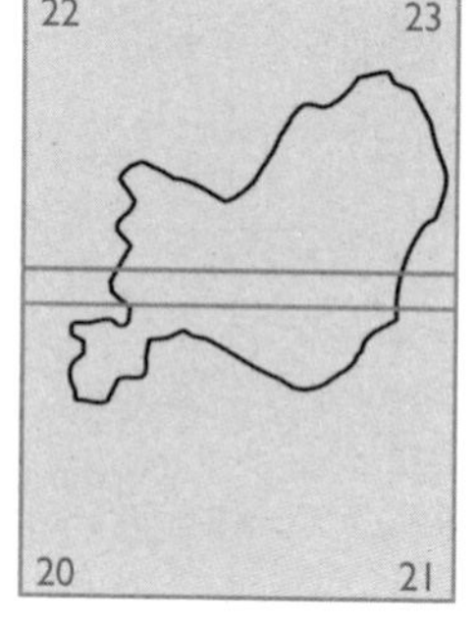

An exploration of the southern end of the Vale of the Severn. The ride starts from the attractive town of Thornbury and goes as far north as Berkeley, with its famous castle and museums. The route is an essentially flat ride through lush pastures, passing stone-built houses with old red tiles weathered green by age. There are good views across the Severn to the Forest of Dean and Wales at several points, notably at Shepperdine.

Start

The High St, Thornbury

P Long-term parking at the back of the supermarket (follow signs)

Distance and grade

33 miles

Easy

Terrain

Mainly flat or undulating in the Vale of the Severn, with one steep hill from Olveston to Old Down

Nearest railway

Yate, 5 miles from the route at Tytherington, or Severn Beach, 6 miles from the route at Olveston. (These stations are not open on Sundays.) Alternatively, Bristol Parkway, 8 miles from Tytherington

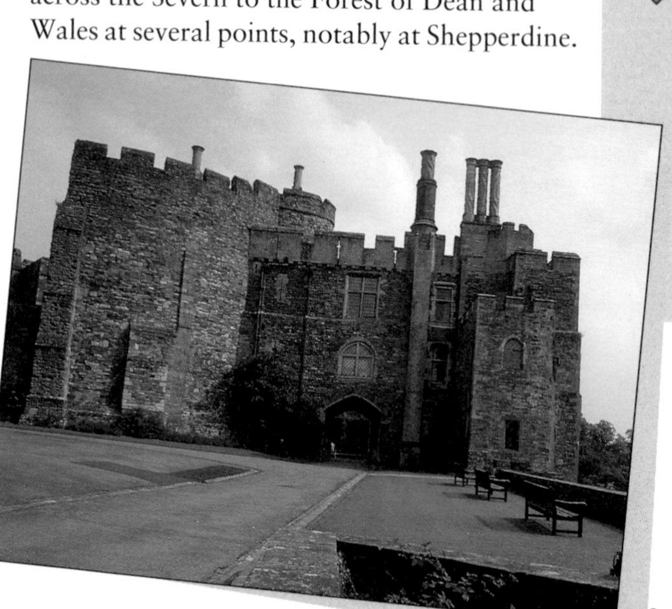

◄ *Berkeley Castle*

Thornbury Tytherington Townwell Berkeley

Places of interest

Berkeley *15*
A quiet Georgian town dominated by the castle, Berkeley also has a fine early English church which contains many memorials to the Berkeley family. The churchyard contains the grave of Edward Jenner (1749-1823) pioneer of smallpox vaccination who was born here.

Berkeley Castle *15*
Situated south of the town of Berkeley this Norman fortress, built in the reign of Henry II, has been transformed into a magnificent stately home surrounded by terraced Elizabethan gardens. It has been the ancestral home of the Berkeley family for over 800 years. A butterfly farm set in a walled garden houses many species of exotic and British butterflies.

Refreshments

White Hart PH ♦♦, ***Littleton-upon-Severn***
The Anchor PH ♦♦, ***Oldbury-on-Severn***
The Swan PH ♦, ***Tytherington***
The Windbound PH ♦, ***Shepperdine***
Plenty of choice in ***Berkeley***
Tea and coffee at Old Down Kitchen Garden, ***Tockington***

The Kitchen Garden, Old Down House, Tockington *26*
Victorian estate with restaurant, country food shop and gift shop. Old Down House is the centre of a mixed dairy and arable farm with the Kitchen Garden Restaurant situated in converted stables.

The Jenner Museum *15*
Museum and medical centre established by the Jenner Trust and British Society for Immunology in memory of Edward Jenner medical scientist and naturalist who discovered the smallpox vaccine after recognising the link between cowpox and smallpox.

Shepperdine
Oldbury-on-Severn
Littleton-upon-Severn
Olveston
Old Down

Churnmead Fm
Park Fm
Cowhill
Kington Ho
Thornbury Park
Littleton Warth
North Field
Castle
Sch
Stock Fm
St Arild's Ho
Lodge Fm
Titters Hill
Kington
Cemy
Rusholme
PH
THORNBURY
Hospl
Cote Fm
Littleton -upon Severn
Sch
Mus
Manor Fm
Hay Wood
Marlwood Fm
Indust Estate
Water Wks
Henley Hill
Resr
Leisure Centre
Gate Fm
Marlwood Grange
Red Hill
Elberton
The Chalet
Sch
Priestpool
Fort
Tumulus
Alveston
Hotel
B4461
Alveston Down
Valley Fm
Hazel Fm
Ingst
New Leaze
Old Down
Stroud Common
MS
Green Hill
Ingst Rhine
Olveston Common
A 38
PH
Lower Hazel
Hayward
Court
Old Down
MS
The Loans
Catherine Hill
Olveston
Sheepcombe Fm
PH
Mead Fm
Sch
Rudgeway
Lodge Fm
Tockington
Church
Pear Tree Fm
Oakleaze
MS
Awkley
M4
The Roundabout
Ostbridge Manor Fm
Harts
Tockington Park Fm
B4427
Angers Fm
The Niatts
Woodhouse Down
Pilning Fm
Fernhill Fm
Hortham Wood
Ringhurst Fm
M5
Cemy
Hortham Fm
Lower Court Fm
Almondsbury
Gaunt's Earthcott
Lower Knole Fm
Hospl
Chapel (rems of)
Inn
Frogland Cross
Cattybrook Fm
Fort
Wks
B4055
Woodlands
North Woods
Tunnel
Over
Sch
Bowsland Fm
The Grange
Court
Patchway
Savage's Wood
BRADLEY STOKE
Chapel (rems of)
Little Stoke

1 From the High Street, follow signs for Gloucester (A38). At roundabout by the Royal George PH turn R past the Plough PH onto Quaker Lane. After 300 yards L by car park onto Gillingstool 'Grovesend, Gloucester'

2 *At roundabout SA 'Gloucester, Bristol (A38)'*

3 *At T-j with A38, L then 1st R 'Quarry ½, Tytherington'*

4 *Opposite The Swan PH in Tytherington L onto Baden Hill Road (NS)*

5 *At T-j R (NS)*

6 *At next T-j L 'Cromhall'*

7 ***Easy to miss****. After ½ mile 1st L*

8 *At X-roads with B4058 L then L again 'Parkend'*

9 *At T-j R (NS). At next T-j L (NS)*

page 22

22 *1½ miles after Oldbury on sharp LH bend by triangle of grass (Thornbury and Kington signposted to the left) turn R*

23 *Ignore 1st L to Olveston and Elberton. Take 2nd L by triangle of grass (same sign). Go past White Hart PH in Littleton*

24 *At offset X-roads with B4461 R then L*

25 *At T-j in Olveston L then L uphill opposite White Hart PH on Vicarage Lane*

26 *Steep climb. At T-j at top of hill L then L again on Foxholes Lane 'Elberton 1½'. 400 yards on left, Old Down Kitchen Garden Tea Shop and Restaurant – well worth a visit!*

27 *At T-j with busy road (B4461) R for ½ mile then 1st L 'Kington, Mumbleys'*

28 *At T-j R (NS)*

29 *After 1 mile at next T-j R 'Thornbury Centre'*

9 *At T-j R (NS). At next T-j L (NS)*

10 *Climb then descend. Opposite black and white lodge house for the prison on the left bear R (B4509) SA 'Tortworth Church'*

11 *Steeply downhill to T-j, R 'North Nibley'*

12 *Continue on this road for 3½ miles following signs for Wick, Berkeley and Newport. At T-j with A38 R then L 'Berkeley Castle 1½'*

13 *At T-j with B4066 L 'Berkeley ½, Sharpness 4'*

14 *At roundabout SA into Berkeley (the castle is on left)*

15 *In the centre of Berkeley, just past the Berkeley Arms PH on your left turn L onto High Street 'Jenners Museum'*

16 *After ¾ mile, shortly after passing Salutation Inn, on sharp LH bend R 'Clapton, Bevington Hill'*

17 *Follow signs for Shepperdine. After 6 miles, at T-j R 'The River, The Windbound'. Fine views of estuary.*

18 *Retrace route for 200 yards, then follow signs for Shepperdine*

19 *At T-j R 'Oldbury 1¼, Thornbury 3½'*

20 *At X-roads SA 'Oldbury Village'*

21 *At T-j R 'Oldbury, Cowhill'. Through Oldbury (The Anchor PH)*

page 21

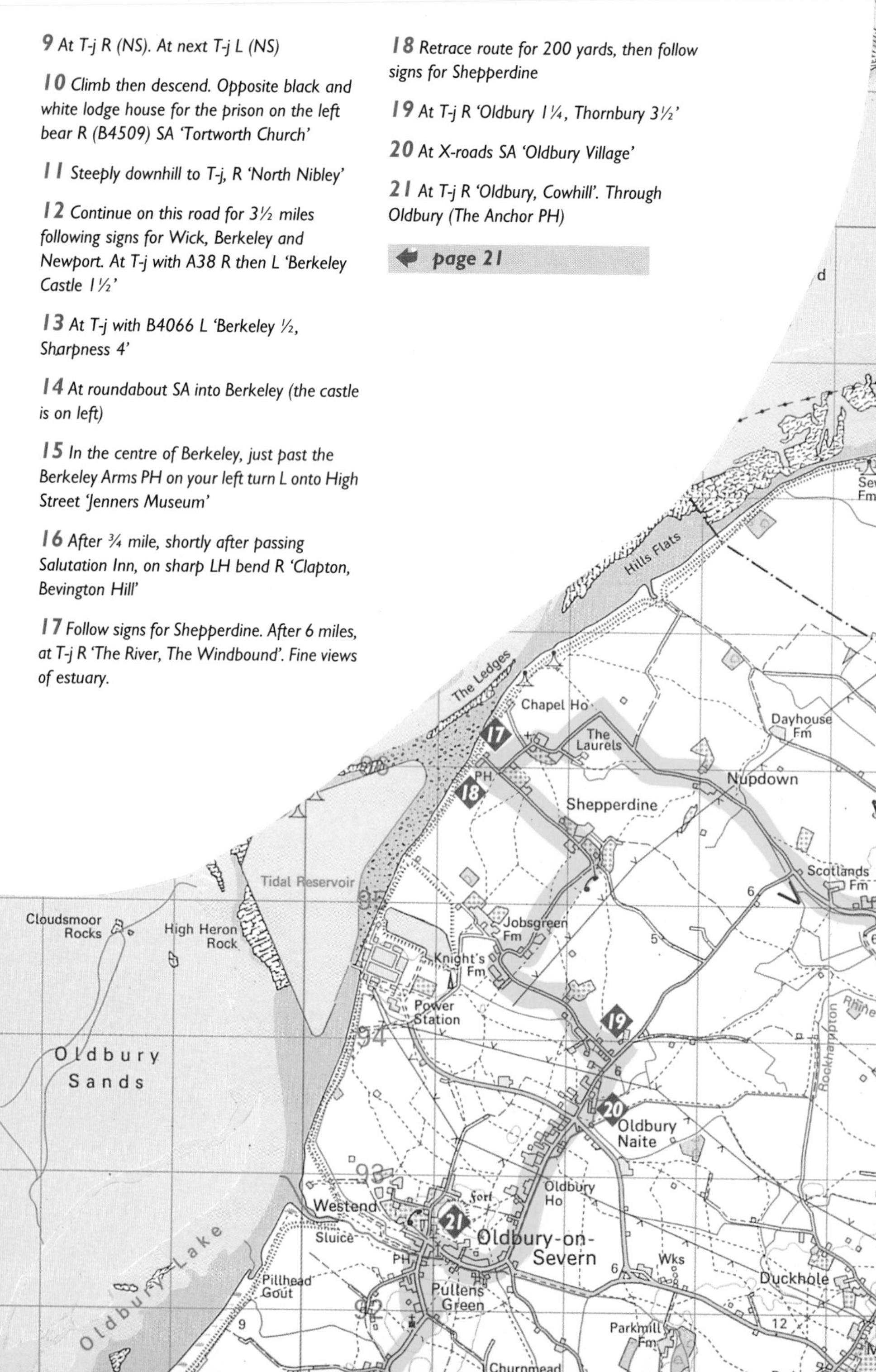

Berkeley
Wanswell
Breadstone
Hook Street
Berkeley Heath
Ham
Newport
Bevington
Whitcliff Park (Deer Park)
Upper Hill
Hystfield
Woodford
Stone
Michael Wood
Damery
Avening Green
Tortworth
Falfield
Rockhampton
Newton
Upper Morton
Leyhill
Lower Stone
Moorslade
Sundayshill
Swanley
Lower Wick
Heathfield
Saniger Sands
Power Station
Eastwood Park
HM Young Offender Institution
H M Prison

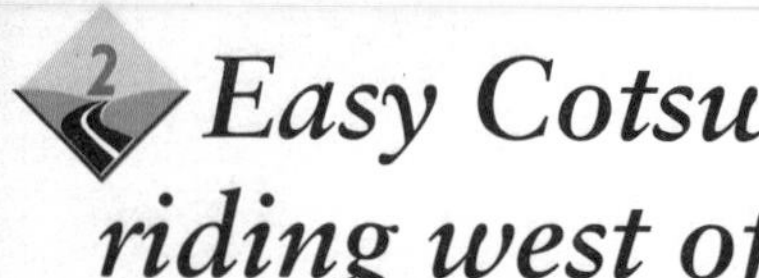

Easy Cotswold riding west of Malmesbury

The route for this easy ride takes in the two prosperous Cotswold towns of Malmesbury and Tetbury and several small villages with beautiful stone buildings. The ride can easily be linked with the east of Malmesbury ride to form a 57-mile loop. Alternatively, Malmesbury can be used as a weekend base to do one ride each day.

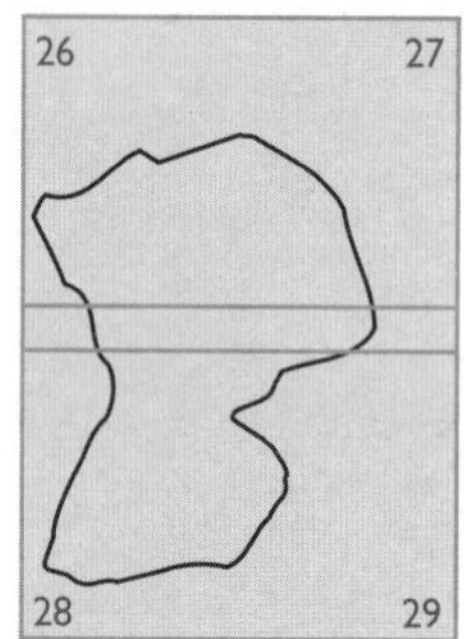

Start

Market cross in the centre of Malmesbury

P Long-term car parks can be found by taking the B4040 Bristol road out of the centre of Malmesbury and following signs for New Station car park

Distance and grade

28 miles

Easy

Terrain

Rolling or flat, no serious hills

Nearest railway

Kemble, 5 miles north of Malmesbury

Refreshments

Suffolk Arms PH, plenty of choice in ***Malmesbury***
Vine Tree PH, ***Norton***
The Crown PH, ***Tetbury***
Plenty of choice in ***Sherston***
Star Inn, Queens Head PH, ***Hullavington***

Malmesbury

Tetbury

Sher

Places of interest

Malmesbury 1

Positioned on the upper reaches of the Avon this is the oldest borough in England. It owes its prosperity to the weaving industry which flourished in the 15th century and many weavers' houses built of Cotswold stone can still be seen. The market cross that dates from 1490 is one of the finest in England.

Malmesbury Abbey 1

This great abbey made the town famous with its foundation in the 7th century. A major part of the later Norman building survives today. The richly carved south porch is particularly outstanding and a musicians' gallery is situated above the nave arcade.

Tetbury 3

Pre-historic Tetbury was the site of a hill fort later taken by the Romans. Through the Middle Ages it prospered as a wool and yarn market selling wool from the Cotswold hill sheep. The pillared Elizabethan market hall is thought to have been the place where local merchants brought their wool to be weighed. Fine merchants' houses and craftsmens' cottages remain and there is a variety of restaurants, tea rooms and specialist shops.

Westonbirt Arboretum 6

Internationally famous, the arboretum has one of the finest and largest collections of trees in the world. Managed by the Forestry Commission since 1956 it has some 17,000 trees and shrubs.

▲ *Market Hall, Tetbury*

Alderton

Grittleton

Hullavington

Foxley

1 *With back to the Market Cross R towards the church, abbey and a large traffic mirror (!). At T-j by memorial cross R past Three Cups PH. Follow signs for Tetbury through three roundabouts, bearing L onto the B4014 at the third*

2 *Bear L again at T-j, following signs for Tetbury. This is the one stretch of the ride where you are not on quiet lanes, which start near Tetbury, so* ***take care***

3 *In Tetbury bear R at the Market Hall 'Dursley, Stroud'*

4 *After 400 yards, L on the A4135 'Dursley, Stroud'*

5 *After ¾ mile, on RH bend, L 'Leighterton 4'*

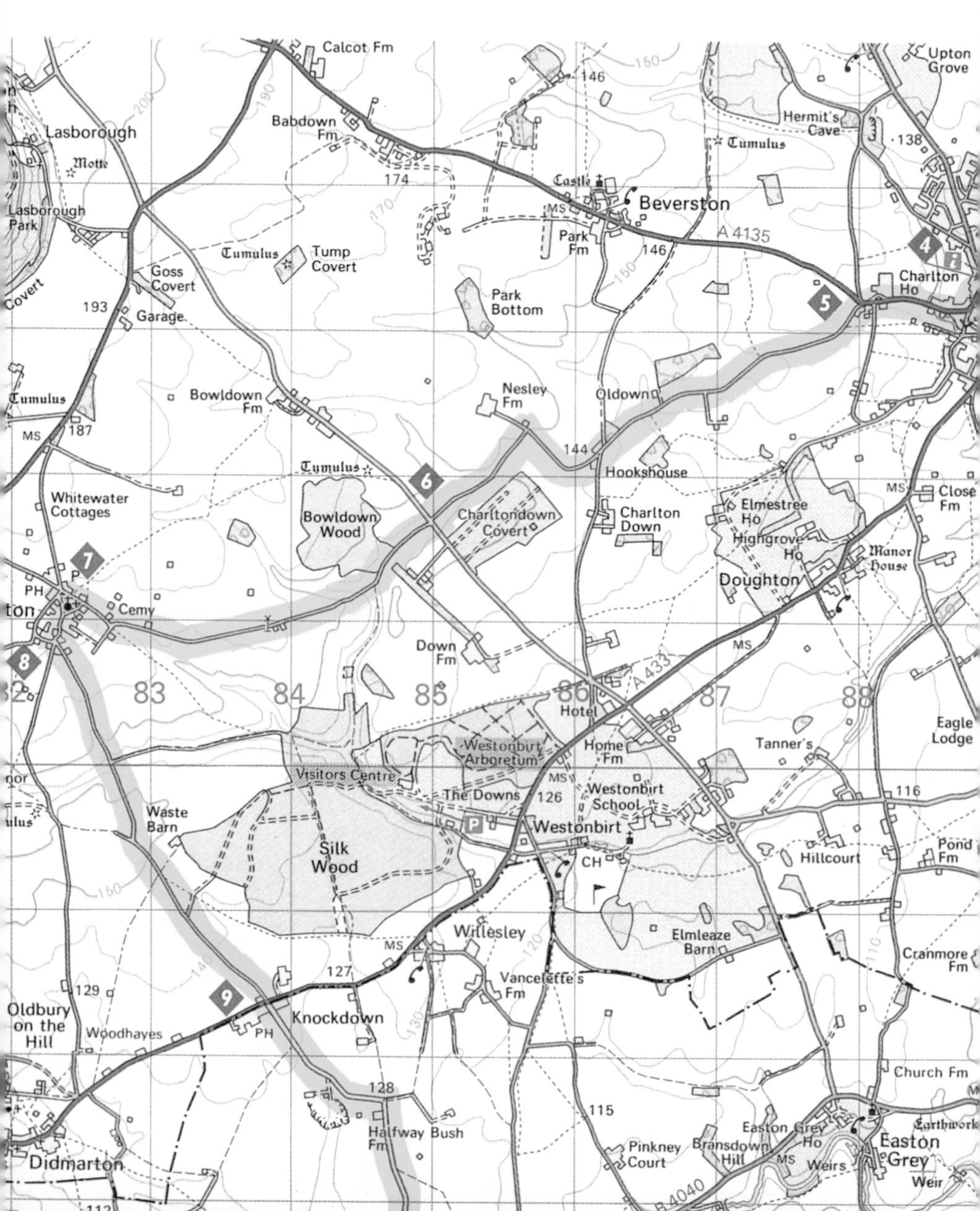

6 SA at X-roads 'Leighterton'

7 Immediately after Royal Oak PH in Leighterton L 'Knockdown 2, Didmarton 2'

8 Soon after PH bear L, passing church on left, then at X-roads L 'Knockdown 2'

9 At X-roads with A433 SA 'Sherston 2'

page 29

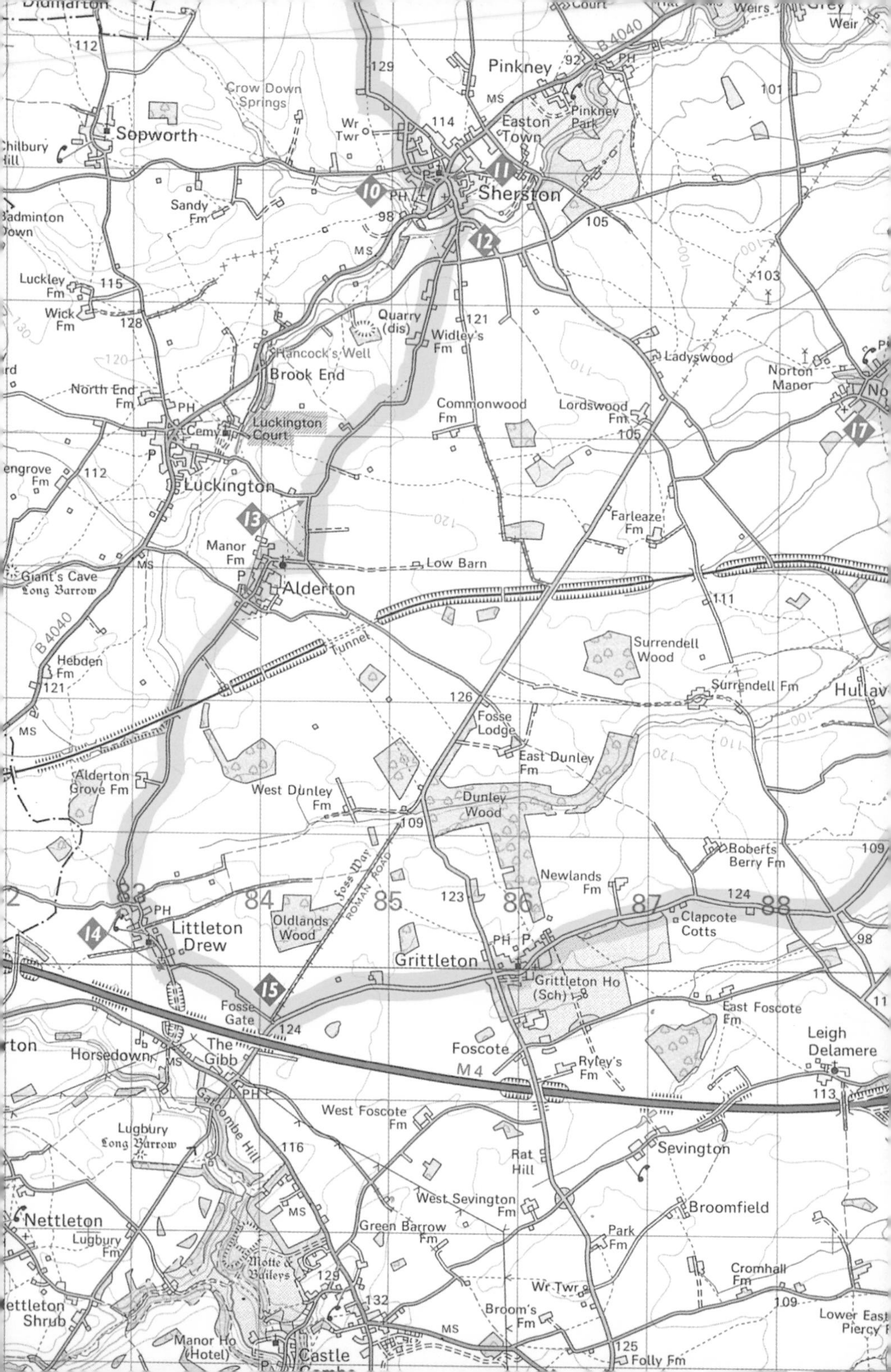

Pinkney
Easton
Town
Pinkney
Park
Sherston
Sopworth
Chilbury
Hill
Crow Down
Springs
Wr
Twr
Sandy
Fm
Badminton
Down
Luckley
Fm
Wick
Fm
Quarry
(dis)
Widley's
Fm
Hancock's Well
Brook End
Ladyswood
Norton
Manor
North End
Fm
Luckington
Court
Commonwood
Fm
Lordswood
Fm
Luckington
Farleaze
Fm
Manor
Fm
Low Barn
Giant's Cave
Long Barrow
Alderton
Tunnel
Hebden
Fm
Surrendell
Wood
Surrendell Fm
Fosse
Lodge
East Dunley
Fm
Alderton
Grove Fm
West Dunley
Fm
Dunley
Wood
Roberts
Berry Fm
Newlands
Fm
Fosse Way
ROMAN ROAD
Clapcote
Cotts
Littleton
Drew
Oldlands
Wood
Grittleton
Grittleton Ho
(Sch)
Fosse
Gate
East Foscote
Fm
Leigh
Delamere
Horsedown
The
Gibb
Foscote
Ryley's
Fm
M 4
West Foscote
Fm
Lugbury
Long Barrow
Gatcombe Hill
Rat
Hill
Sevington
Nettleton
West Sevington
Fm
Broomfield
Lugbury
Fm
Green Barrow
Fm
Park
Fm
Motte &
Baileys
Cromhall
Fm
Wr Twr
Broom's
Fm
Lower East
Piercy
Manor Ho
(Hotel)
Castle
Folly Fm
Weirs
Weir
B4040
10
11
12
13
14
15
17
83
84
85
86
87
88

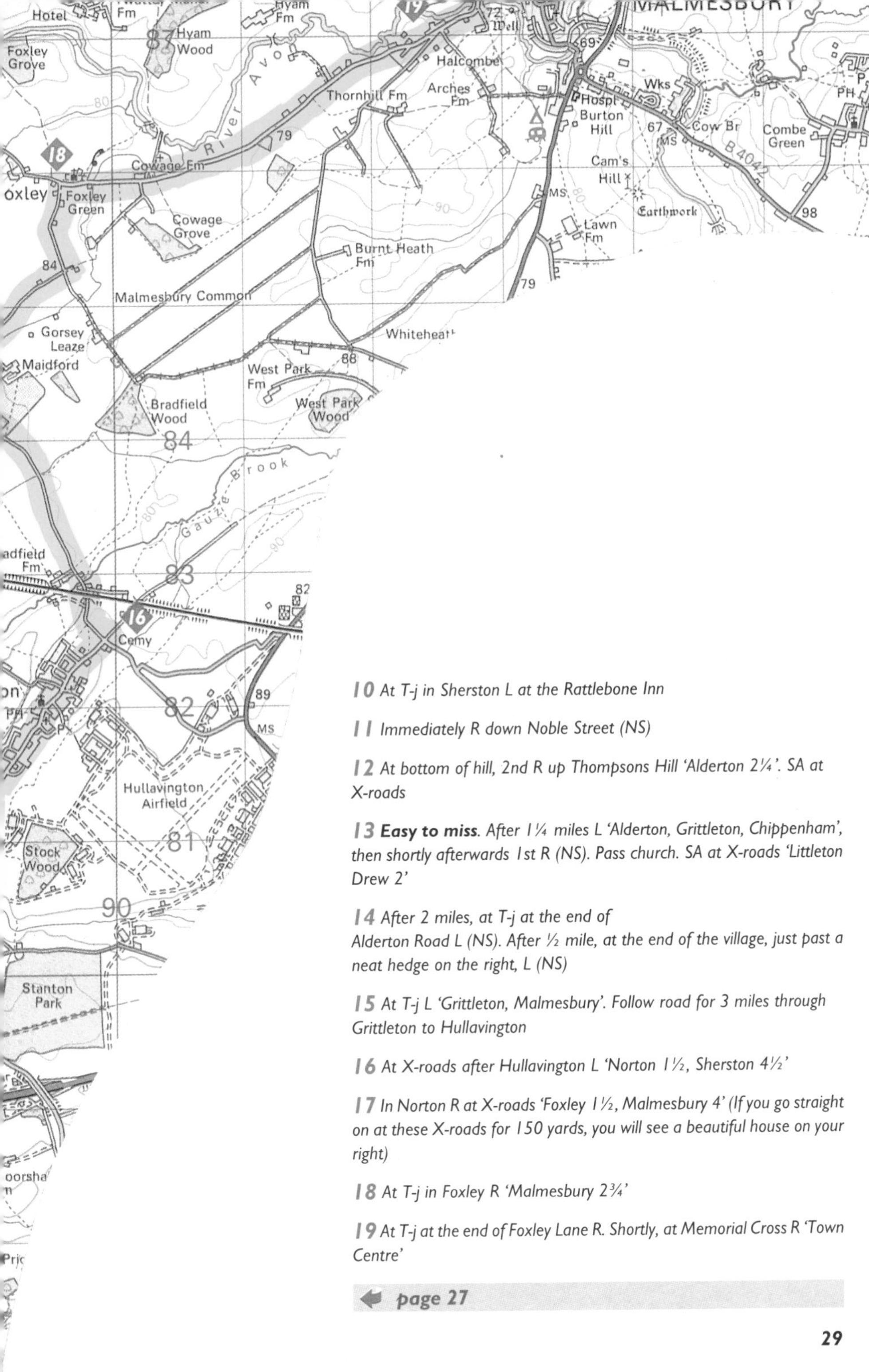

10 *At T-j in Sherston L at the Rattlebone Inn*

11 *Immediately R down Noble Street (NS)*

12 *At bottom of hill, 2nd R up Thompsons Hill 'Alderton 2¼'. SA at X-roads*

13 ***Easy to miss**. After 1¼ miles L 'Alderton, Grittleton, Chippenham', then shortly afterwards 1st R (NS). Pass church. SA at X-roads 'Littleton Drew 2'*

14 *After 2 miles, at T-j at the end of Alderton Road L (NS). After ½ mile, at the end of the village, just past a neat hedge on the right, L (NS)*

15 *At T-j L 'Grittleton, Malmesbury'. Follow road for 3 miles through Grittleton to Hullavington*

16 *At X-roads after Hullavington L 'Norton 1½, Sherston 4½'*

17 *In Norton R at X-roads 'Foxley 1½, Malmesbury 4' (If you go straight on at these X-roads for 150 yards, you will see a beautiful house on your right)*

18 *At T-j in Foxley R 'Malmesbury 2¾'*

19 *At T-j at the end of Foxley Lane R. Shortly, at Memorial Cross R 'Town Centre'*

page 27

3 *Easy Cotswold riding east of Malmesbury*

The route east of Malmesbury provides an easy ride through small villages and along quiet lanes. It crosses the River Avon twice before climbing out of the valley at Little Somerford and continuing east towards the lovely woods of Somerford Common – a good place for a picnic. Should you wish someone else to prepare your lunch for you, the Wheatsheaf Inn in Oaksey is a fine country pub.

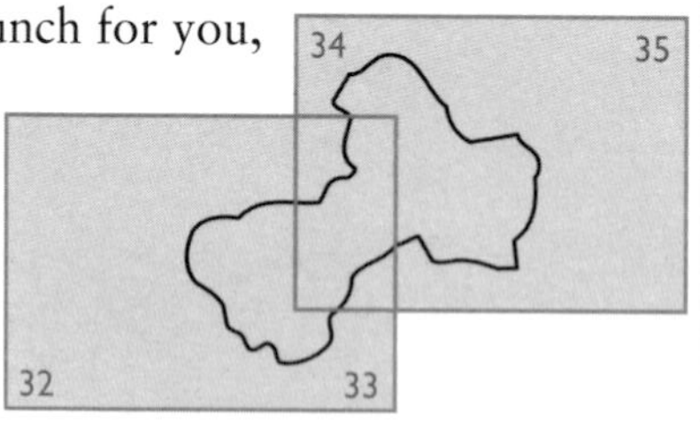

Start

Market cross in the centre of Malmesbury

P Long-term car parks can be found by taking the B4040 Bristol road out of the centre of Malmesbury and following signs for New Station car park

Distance and grade

29 miles
Easy

Terrain

Rolling or flat, no serious hills

Nearest railway

Kemble, 5 miles north of Malmesbury

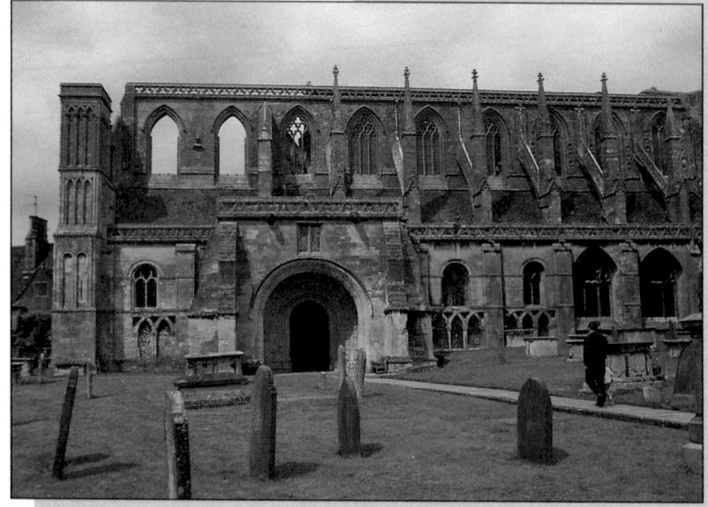

► *Malmesbury Abbey*

Malmesbury
Corston
Startley
Great Somerford
Little Somerford

Places of interest

Malmesbury *1*
Many famous names are associated with Malmesbury: St Aldhelm (656-709); King Athelstan who gave the town its royal heath; William of Malmesbury, a great historian of the Middle Ages and the philosopher Thomas Hobbes (1588-1679).

Elmer of Malmesbury – the Flying Monk
In 1010 AD Elmer, a Saxon monk, climbed to the top of Malmesbury Abbey Tower and attempted to fly with the wings he had made. This flight lasted more than 620 feet but on landing he broke both legs. A window in the abbey recalls this event.

Oaksey *15*
On the border with Gloucestershire, the parish contains Norwood Castle a Norman earthwork scheduled as an ancient monument. The village has Tudor and 17th-century houses and the church has some interesting 15th-century wall paintings uncovered in 1933.

Refreshments

Volunteer Inn, ***Great Somerford***
Little Somerford Arms PH, ***Little Somerford***
Turnpike Arms PH, ***Minety***
Horse and Groom PH, ***Charlton***
Three Crowns PH, ***Brinkworth***
The Wheatsheaf PH, ***Oaksey***

Minety
Upper Minety
Oaksey
Charlton

1 With back to the Market Cross R towards the church, abbey and a large traffic mirror (!). At T-j by Memorial Cross L 'Sherston B4040'

2 1st L, 'Foxley 2, Norton 3½'. Cross bridge over River Avon. Climb hill and bear L after 400 yards 'Common Road to Corston'

3 After 2 miles, at T-j with A429 R, then L opposite Radnor Arms PH on to Rodbourne Road. **Take care!** This is a busy road and it may be best to cross the road and push your bike along the pavement for 200 yards as far as Rodbourne Road

4 Shortly after passing octagonal communications tower on your left in Rodbourne, next R 'Rodbourne Bottom, Cleeve House'. At T-j with Oakdene Cottage opposite R

5 After ¾ mile, 1st L in Startley 'Great Somerford 1¼, Dauntsey 3½'

6 At X-roads in Great Somerford L 'Little Somerford, Malmesbury'

7 After 1½ miles at T-j in Little Somerford L then immediately R onto Clay Street

8 At T-j with main road (B4042) R 'Swindon 13', then L 'Cleverton, Minety'

➡ **page 35**

19 At T-j (with B4040) in Charlton at the end of Vicarage Lane R 'Malmesbury'

20 Through village. Shortly after the end of the houses, before a signposted RH bend turn L 'Garsdon 1, Lea 1½'

21 After ¾ mile at X-roads (your priority) R 'Malmesbury'

22 After 1¼ miles on sharp RH bend by a telephone box bear L (in effect SA) onto No Through Road 'Wiltshire Cycleway'

23 At X-roads with A429 SA on to Blicks Lane

24 At T-j opposite Duke of York PH L into Malmesbury

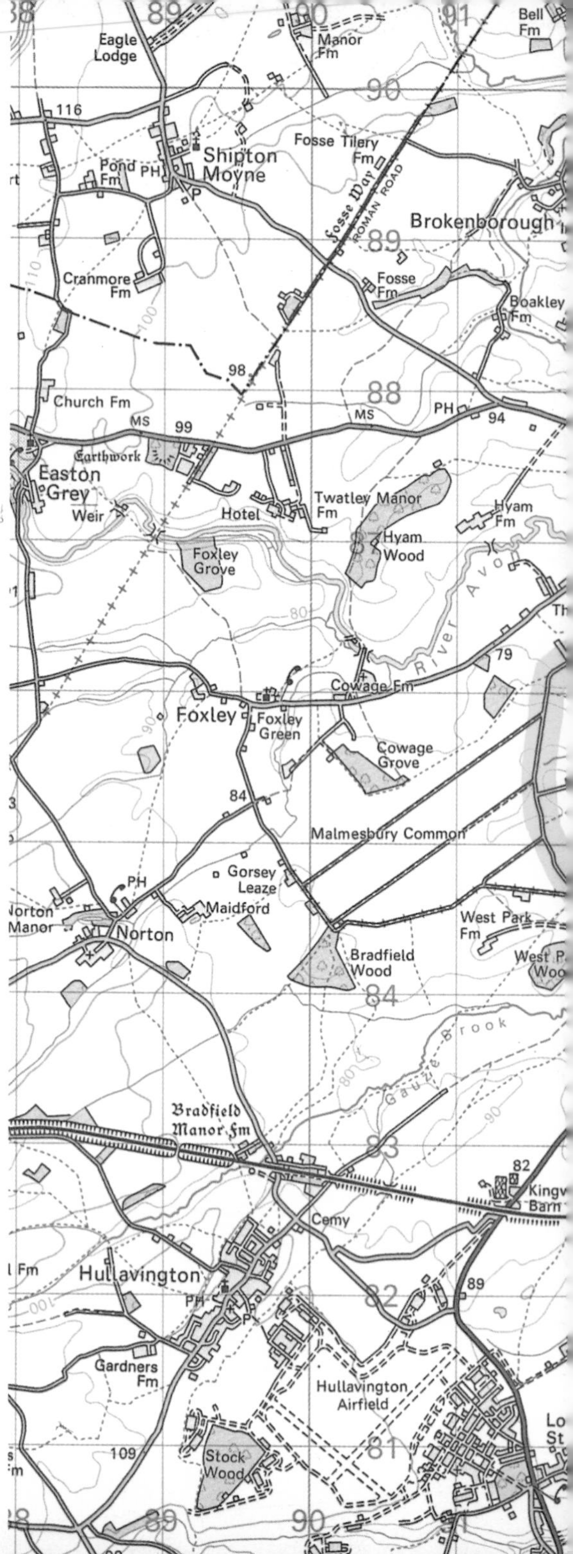

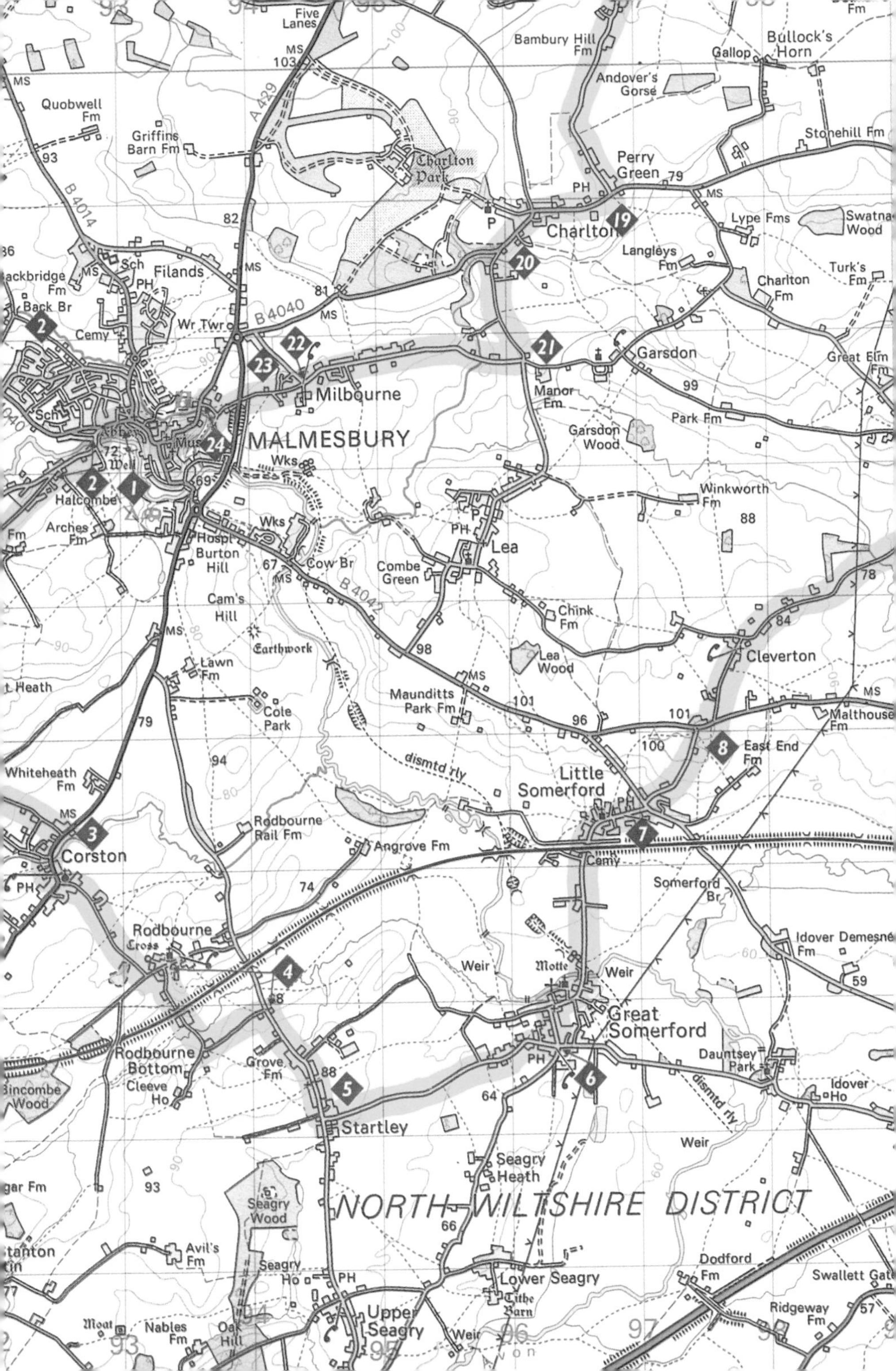
MALMESBURY
Charlton
Charlton Park
Perry Green
Garsdon
Milbourne
Filands
Lea
Cleverton
Little Somerford
Great Somerford
Corston
Rodbourne
Rodbourne Bottom
Startley
Seagry Heath
Lower Seagry
Upper Seagry
Five Lanes
Bambury Hill Fm
Bullock's Horn
Gallop
Andover's Gorse
Stonehill Fm
Quobwell Fm
Griffins Barn Fm
Lype Fms
Swatnage Wood
Langleys Fm
Charlton Fm
Turk's Fm
Great Elm Fm
Manor Fm
Park Fm
Garsdon Wood
Winkworth Fm
Combe Green
Chink Fm
Lea Wood
Maunditts Park Fm
Malthouse Fm
East End Fm
Halcombe
Arches Fm
Burton Hill
Cam's Hill
Earthwork
Lawn Fm
Cole Park
Whiteheath Fm
Rodbourne Rail Fm
Angrove Fm
Somerford Br
Idover Demesne Fm
Motte
Weir
Dauntsey Park
Idover Ho
Grove Fm
Cleeve Ho
Bincombe Wood
Seagry Wood
Seagry Ho
Avil's Fm
Tithe Barn
Moat
Nables Fm
Oak Hill
Dodford Fm
Swallett Gate
Ridgeway Fm
Cow Br
Back Br
Cemy
Wr Twr
Wks
Hospl
Abbey
Mus
Well
dismtd rly
NORTH WILTSHIRE DISTRICT
A 429
B 4014
B 4040
B 4042
1
2
3
4
5
6
7
8
19
20
21
22
23
24

Dean Plantation
Motte & Bailey
Country Park
Chelworth Lawns
Laynes Fm
Dean Fm
Lowfield Fm
Oaksey Moor Fm
Gravel Pit
Chelworth
Lower Moor Fm
Oaksey Wood
Oaksey
Gravel Pit
Nature Trail
Clattinger Fm
Crudwell
Flintham Ho
Eastcourt
Park Fm
Stert Fm
Cooles Fm
Lyngrove Fm
Eastcourt Ho
Braydon Brook Fm
Oaksey Nursery
Brandier
Rookery Fm
Flisteridge Wood
Hankerton Field Fm
Upper Minety
Hankerton
Cloatley
The Elms
Dolman's Fm
Cloatley End
Bambury Hill Fm
Bullock's Horn
Woodward Fm
Andover's Gorse
Park Copse
Stonehill Fm
Charlton Park
Perry Green
Stonehill Wood
Stone Hill
Summer House Fm
B 4040
Charlton
Lype Fms
Swatnage Wood
Turk's Fm
Pond Fm
Nineteen Acre Wood
Great Withy Wood
Garsdon
Worthy Hill Fm
Great Elm Fm
Braydon Pond
Park Fm
Garsdon Wood
Braydon Wood
Winkworth Fm
Somerford Fm
Lea
Wood Hill
Sundays Hill Fm
Chink Fm
Woodbridge Brook
Braydon Side
Lea Wood
Cleverton
Weeks Fm
Ramps Hill
Malthouse Fm
Lodge Fm
B 4042
Little Somerford
Causeway End
Cemy

8 *At T-j with main road (B4042) R 'Swindon 13', then L, 'Cleverton, Minety'*

9 *At T-j R 'Brinkworth, Wootton Bassett'*

10 *At T-j L 'Minety 3½'*

11 *At offset X-roads R then L 'Minety 2½, Purton 4½'*

12 *At T-j L 'Minety'*

13 *At X-roads with B4040 SA into Minety*

14 *After almost 2 miles, on gentle LH bend in Upper Minety, R 'Minety Church, Oaksey 2'*

15 *At X-roads in Oaksey SA for the Wheatsheaf Inn or L 'Crudwell, Culkerton, Malmesbury' to continue route*

16 *At mini-roundabout by Post Office at the end of Oaksey village 'Eastcourt'*

17 *At X-roads SA 'Hankerton, Charlton, Malmesbury'*

18 *At T-j L 'Hankerton, Charlton'*

19 *At T-j (with B4040) in Charlton at the end of Vicarage Lane R 'Malmesbury'*

20 *Through village. Shortly after the end of the houses, before a signposted RH bend turn L 'Garsdon 1, Lea 1½'*

21 *After ¾ mile at X-roads (your priority) R 'Malmesbury 2'*

page 32

4 From Clifton to Clevedon, west of Bristol

To explore one of Bristol's best escapes into the countryside begin by crossing the Avon Gorge via the Clifton Suspension Bridge; after a mile on the A369 you plunge into a network of small country lanes that lead to the impressive church at Lower Failand with good views across to the Bristol Channel.

A swift descent down a narrow lane brings you to Portbury and the start of the section along the Gordano Valley.

About 5 miles on from Portbury the route climbs out of the valley and up onto the ridge between Portishead and Clevedon, with fine views out across the Bristol Channel to Wales.

Continue across Clevedon Moor and Kenn Moor gathering strength on this flat section for the major climb of the ride up through the thickly wooded Brockley Combe.

The final stage of the ride takes you through Long Ashton and Ashton Court, a pleasant way to regain height back up to the suspension bridge.

Start

Clifton Suspension Bridge, west of Bristol

P Towards or on the Downs, north of the Bridge

Distance and grade

32 miles

Moderate

Terrain

Mainly undulating, through a variety of scenery. One long hill, (430 feet over 3 miles) up onto Lulsgate and three short steep ones (before Failand, before Clevedon, and after Barrow Gurney)

Nearest railway

Bristol Temple Meads. Alternatively, Yatton is 3 miles from the route at Kenn Moor

Refreshments

*Black Horse PH, **Clapton in Gordano***
*Plenty of choice in **Clevedon***
*Blue Flame PH, **West End** (east of Clevedon)*
*Princes Motto PH, **Barrow Gurney***

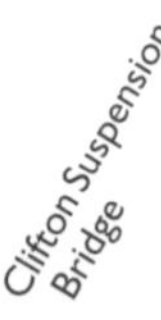

Places of interest

***Clifton Suspension Bridge** 1*
The distinctive landmark stands 245 feet above high water and has a total span of 702 feet. Work started on the bridge in 1836, based on a design by Isambard Kingdom Brunel but it was not officially opened until 1864. The most famous story concerning the bridge is that of Sarah Ann Henley. In 1885 she jumped off the bridge after a quarrel with her lover and was gently parachuted by her petticoats to the mud below.

***Avon Gorge Nature Reserve** 2*
Leigh Woods is beautiful woodland owned by the National Trust. The gorge is cut out of limestone and is famous for rare trees and flowers.

***Clevedon** 12*
A quiet seaside town that has retained much of its earlier Victorian charm, Clevedon lies on a part of the Bristol Channel known for its high tides which caused the pier to collapse in 1970.

***Clevedon Court** 16*
This 14th-century manor house was once fortified and is one of the oldest of its type to have survived anywhere in Britain. It is still the home of the Elton family whose outstanding collection of family portraits, 19th-century Eltonware pottery and Nailsea glass are on show.

Short cuts

***For a 13-mile ride** at instruction 8, just before Clapton-in-Gordano, L instead of R, cross the bridge over the M5 and climb steeply to the B3128 and B3129 to return via Failand to the suspension bridge*

***For a 22-mile ride** go as far as Clevedon, but at instruction 16 go SA and return directly via Tickenham and Failand, taking the B3130, B3128 and B3129*

Extensions

After Clevedon, between instructions 17 and 18, take the 1st R and head for the Mendips via Yatton, Wrington and Burrington

After crossing the A38 near Lulsgate, after instruction 21 and before 22, follow the Avon Cycleway from Felton via Chew Stoke, Pensford, Compton Dando to Saltford to return to Bristol via the Bristol and Bath Cyclepath. If you need to return to the suspension bridge, you will have to cross the centre of Bristol. This longer ride is about 50 miles

***Clevedon Craft Centre and Countryside Museum** 16*
Situated in the grounds of Clevedon Court. Here you can watch the craftsmen at work in a rural atmosphere. There are over 12 studios with high quality crafts for sale and a tea room for refreshments.

Barrow Gurney

Long Ashton

Middle Bridge
PH
6
P
Priory
GORDANO
Pill
Hospl
Ham Green
Sch
Easton-in-Gordano
PH
Portbury
Settlement
The Mount
Markham Fm
Upper Caswell Fm
Caswell Cross
7
5
14
8
Prior's Wood
Happerton Fms
42
Haberfield Park Fm
Windmill Hill
120
56
97
Charlton Fm
Sch
Lower Failand
4
Naish Ho
Moat House Fm
Old Hill
Failand Hill Ho
Failand Ho
Glen Fm
144
136
128
B 3128
149
Failand Fm
West Hill
81
Wraxall Court
Failand Lodge Fm
Homestead
159
P
PH
147
CH
Birdcombe Court
Wraxall
52
MP
Wraxall Ho
B 3130
PH
Tyntesfield
142
Longwood Ho
149
Tyntesfield Plantn
Failand
CH
48
Land Yeo
Belmont Ho
Ashton Hill Plantn
Gable Fm
87
P
Sch
Brook Fm
East End
28
27
Backwell Common
Depot
33
ROMAN SETTLEMENT
MP
Hospl
Backwell Green
P
34
Inn
54
Cambridge Batch
Farleigh
MS
52
Flax Bourton
Backwell Ho
Redwood Fm
Sch
A 370
Bourton Combe
MS
P
Backwell
Mill
24
West Town
PH
Barrow Court
Home Fm
B 3130
Barrow Wood
26
PH
Wks
DISTRICT
Cave
155
Barrow Gurney
MS
Backwell Hill
25
Resrs
Chelvey Batch
Barrow Hill
Mon
20
Backwell Hill Ho
179
24
47
Settlement
Hyattswood Fm
Freemans Fm
MP
PH
Yorkhouse Cave
Healls Scars
202
Quarry (dis)
Brockley Combe
The Batch
Wood
Nature Trail
MP
Potters Hill
PH
187
Downside
21
Upper Town
23
P
Felton
22
PH
Wrington Warren
Warren Ho
Lulsgate Bottom
PH

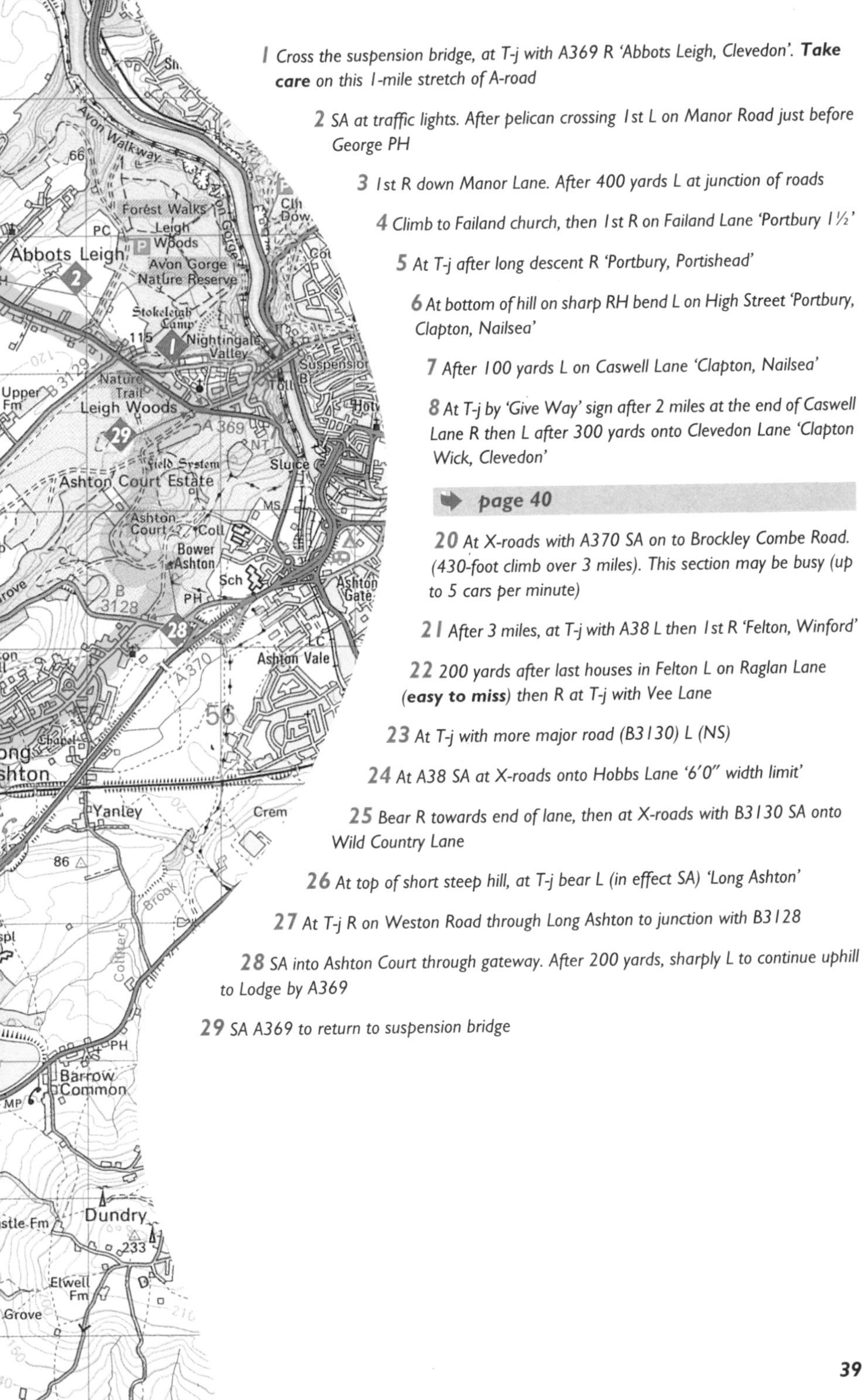

1 *Cross the suspension bridge, at T-j with A369 R 'Abbots Leigh, Clevedon'.* ***Take care*** *on this 1-mile stretch of A-road*

2 *SA at traffic lights. After pelican crossing 1st L on Manor Road just before George PH*

3 *1st R down Manor Lane. After 400 yards L at junction of roads*

4 *Climb to Failand church, then 1st R on Failand Lane 'Portbury 1½'*

5 *At T-j after long descent R 'Portbury, Portishead'*

6 *At bottom of hill on sharp RH bend L on High Street 'Portbury, Clapton, Nailsea'*

7 *After 100 yards L on Caswell Lane 'Clapton, Nailsea'*

8 *At T-j by 'Give Way' sign after 2 miles at the end of Caswell Lane R then L after 300 yards onto Clevedon Lane 'Clapton Wick, Clevedon'*

page 40

20 *At X-roads with A370 SA on to Brockley Combe Road. (430-foot climb over 3 miles). This section may be busy (up to 5 cars per minute)*

21 *After 3 miles, at T-j with A38 L then 1st R 'Felton, Winford'*

22 *200 yards after last houses in Felton L on Raglan Lane (**easy to miss**) then R at T-j with Vee Lane*

23 *At T-j with more major road (B3130) L (NS)*

24 *At A38 SA at X-roads onto Hobbs Lane '6'0" width limit'*

25 *Bear R towards end of lane, then at X-roads with B3130 SA onto Wild Country Lane*

26 *At top of short steep hill, at T-j bear L (in effect SA) 'Long Ashton'*

27 *At T-j R on Weston Road through Long Ashton to junction with B3128*

28 *SA into Ashton Court through gateway. After 200 yards, sharply L to continue uphill to Lodge by A369*

29 *SA A369 to return to suspension bridge*

8 At T-j by 'Give Way' sign after 2 miles at the end of Caswell Lane R then L after 300 yards onto Clevedon Lane 'Clapton Wick, Clevedon'

9 After 4 miles, at T-j with B3124, R on Walton Road 'Walton, Portishead'

10 After 300 yards 1st L 'Walton St. Mary' up Holly Lane which becomes Castle Road then Wellington Terrace

11 ½ mile after the Highcliffe Hotel and opposite church with red tile roof on the left bear R down Marine Parade 'Seafront'

12 At T-j at the end of the promenade (The Beach) R on Elton Road

13 Bear L along Old Church Road. At traffic lights SA past shops to clock tower

14 Bear L, past more shops onto Old Street

15 At roundabout after 1 mile R on B3130 'Nailsea'. Next roundabout SA to B3130 'Nailsea'

16 After 300 yards 1st R onto Court Lane 'Clevedon Craft Centre'

17 ¾ mile after Craft Centre at X-roads by Give Way sign L

18 **Ignore** 1st R on Kenn Moor Road. 1 mile after passing Blue Flame PH on your left take next R '7.5 ton weight limit'

19 Cross railway bridge and pass church on the left. Next R onto Brockley Lane (sign may be obscured by brambles). Follow signs for Brockley Combe

20 At X-roads with A370 SA on to Brockley Combe Road (430-foot climb over 3 miles). This section may be busy (up to 5 cars per minute)

page 39

PORTISHEAD
Portishead Down
Charlcombe Bay
Walton Bay
North Weston
How Ham Fm
Upper Caswell Fm
Middle Bridge
Weston Down
Farley
Walton Down
Weston in Gordano
Clapton in Gordano
Clapton Moor
Clapton Court
Weston Moor
Walton in Gordano
B 3124
New Fm
Naish Ho
Moat House Fm
Clapton Wick
Walton Moor
Norton's Wood
Tickenham Hill
Cadbury Camp
Lime Breach Wood
Hale's Fm
West Hill
Wraxall Court
B 3128
Middletown
Court Hill
Tickenham
Inn
Birdcombe Court
Stone-edge Batch
Court
Cadbury Court Fm
B 3130
Wraxall Ho
Land Yeo
Clevedon Moor
Tickenham Moor
Nailsea Moor
Parish Brook
Sch
East End
Nailsea
Nursebatch Fm
West End
River Kenn
Backwell
Kenn Moor
Manor Fm
Netherton Wood
Chelvey
Nailsea Court
Court
Midgell Fm
West Town
WOODSPRING DISTRICT
Kenn Moor Gate
Brockley Elm Fm
Chelvey Batch
Backwell Hill Ho
Brockley Court
Hall
Brockley
Settlement
Yorkhouse Cave
Hillsea
Laurel Fm
Horsecastle
Claverham
A 370
Brockley Combe
The Batch
Brockley Wood
Cleeve Hill
Yatton
Cleeve
Cleeve Court
Cleeve Toot
Wrington Warren
Warren Ho
8
16
17
18
19
20

5 Bath to Castle Combe and Lacock

The ride out of Bath beside the Kennet and Avon canal to the east takes you along the beautiful towpath to Bathampton then climbs out of the valley into the southern Cotswolds via Marshfield before dropping down to the delights of Castle Combe. Another climb takes you south and east to the equally fascinating village of Lacock. Skirting south of Corsham, the ride climbs steadily to Kingsdown, with magnificent views towards Bath, before dropping into Bathford and a return along the towpath.

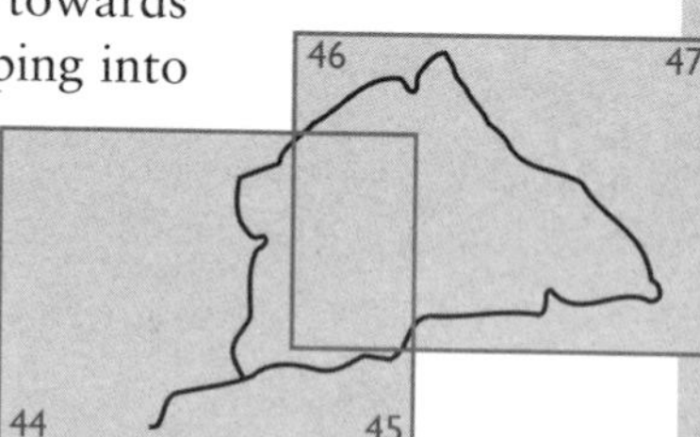

Start

Bath Spa railway station

P If arriving by car, it is better to start and finish at Bathampton, near the George PH and do the route from instructions 5 to 35

Distance and grade

35 miles

Moderate

Terrain

Two climbs of 500 feet, a steep one from Batheaston to Marshfield and a more steady one from Lacock to Kingsdown. Apart from these and two short steep hills near Castle Combe, the ride is generally flat or undulating

Nearest railway

Bath Spa

Bath
Batheaston
Marshfield
Mountain Bower
Castle Combe

Places of interest

***Bath** 1*

The famous Roman baths were built around the natural hot spring which rises from the ground at 46.5°C. The presence of the spring established Bath as a bathing, curative and social centre and remained fashionable in the 18th century. Bath is also famous for its elegant Georgian architecture. The Royal Crescent, the first terrace to be built as a crescent, remains one of the finest examples in Europe. Bath also has numerous museums, a magnificent abbey and an industrial heritage centre.

***Lacock** 23*

A National Trust village of stone and half-timbered houses dating back to the 15th century with none later than 1800.

***Lacock Abbey** 23*

The magnificent Lacock Abbey standing on the banks of the River Avon was founded in 1232 by the Countess of Salisbury. The original cloisters and chapter house survive, but after its supression in 1539 it was converted into a Tudor dwelling house by Sir William Sharrington.

Refreshments

The George PH, plenty of choice in ***Lacock***
Lord Nelson PH, Catherine Wheel PH, ***Marshfield***
Plenty of choice in ***Castle Combe***

***The Fox Talbot Photographic Museum** 23*

The museum is situated in a 16th-century barn near the gates of Lacock Abbey. It displays the work and equipment of W H Fox Talbot, a pioneer of photography who once owned the abbey.

***Castle Combe** 15*

A picturesque village in the wooded Bybrook valley, of Cotswold stone houses with a stone-canopied market cross at the centre. The village was the venue for the film *Doctor Dolittle* in 1966.

***Kennet and Avon Canal** 3 and 36*

Opened by the Queen in 1990, the canal stretches 87 miles between Reading and Bristol passing through 104 locks and over a height of 450 feet.

Lacock
Gastard
Chapel Plaister

1 L out of station, past car hire office, through tunnel to rear of station

2 Walk bike across green bridge over river, L on Rossiter Road

3 After 50 yards L 'Thimble Mill Conference and Banqueting Suite'. Do not cross bridge. Go immediately R alongside canal

4 Follow signs 'Bathampton, Kennet and Avon Canal Towpath' for 2 miles, crossing bridges and changing sides as indicated by signs. This will involve some short flights of steps. You are advised to dismount under the bridges where the path is narrow

5 At George PH leave canal, L over railway bridge then tollbridge over Avon, passing Old Mill Hotel

6 At T-j R on A363 for ½ mile. **Take care** crossing road

7 Shortly after the White Hart PH ignore left turn on 'The Batch'. Take the next L up Penthouse Hill 'North End, St Catherine'

8 Follow this road for 1½ miles ignoring R and L turns until signpost 'Oakford, Marshfield, Colerne'. R downhill to cross stream

9 Long climb, steep at the end. At T-j at the top of Oakford Lane L

10 After 2½ miles at T-j at the end of St Martins Lane in Marshfield turn R, following High Street around LH then RH bend to emerge at A420

11 At T-j with A420 R for ½ mile then 1st L 'West Kington, Nettleton'

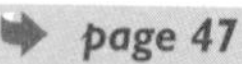
page 47

30 Go down steep hill. At X-roads SA A365 (NS)

31 At T-j by Hatt Farm R. Follow past golf course down into Kingsdown

32 At T-j by Crown PH R on A361 towards railway bridge. Just before bridge, L on footpath (push bike until railway crossing)

33 Fork R up over railway bridge to cross river

34 Over stile, cross field diagonally R to next stile, then with great care SA railway crossing

35 On tarmac track to The George PH at Bathampton. L opposite primary school

36 Retrace route to Bath, following signs 'Kennet and Avon Canal Towpath Bath'

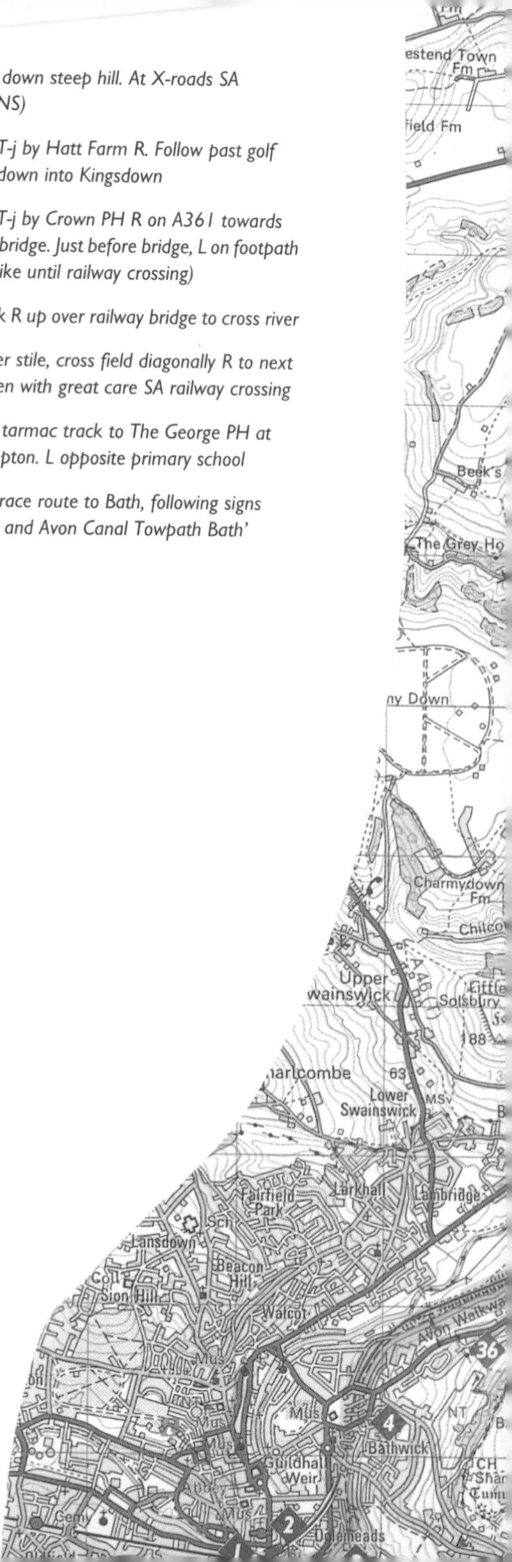

Castle Fm
Cemy
Marshfield
Wraxall
The Shoe
Star Fm
East End
Bury Camp
Cross Dyke
Colerne Down
Fuddlebrook Hill
Henley Hill
Fuddlebrook
Lucknam Park
Hall Fm
Colerne Park
Thickwood
Bks
The Raizes
Ashwicke Grange
Ashwicke Hall (Sch)
Airfield (dis)
Wr Twr
Euridge Manor Fm
Eastrip
Colerne
Widdenham Fm
Nailey Fm
Ayford Fm
Hunters Hall
The Rocks
St Catherine
St Catharine's Court
Three Shire Stones
Oakford Fm
Westwood Fm
ROMAN ROAD
Wks
Folly Fm
Lid Brook
By Brook
Mill
Rodney Fm
Ditteridge
Alcombe
Cheney Court
Fogleigh Ho
Middlehill
Tunnel
Shockerwick Ho
The Hill
Northend
Banner Down
The Mount
Ashley
Box
Hazelbury Manor
Sheylors Fm
Tumuli
Henley
Blue Vein
Batheaston
Box Br
Kingsdown
River Avon
Toll
Weir
Mill
Tumulus
Bathampton
Nature Trail
Bathford
Norbin Fm
Norbin Barton Fm
Brown's Folly
Monkton Farleigh Mine
Holcombe Fm
Bathford Hill
Manor Ho
Monkton Farleigh
Rushmead Fm
Cat's
Bathampton Down
Castle
Fort
Univ
Kennet & Avon Canal
Warleigh Manor
Pump
Warleigh
Pinckney Green
South Wraxall

West Kington
Nettleton Shrub
Motte & Baileys
Castle Combe
Manor Ho (Hotel)
Brook Ho
Broom's Fm
Motor Racing Circuit
West Kington Wick
Shrub Fm
Fosse Fm
Mountain Bower
Truckle Hill
Rack Hill
West Yatton Down
Long Dean
North Wraxall
Ford
West Yatton
Ivy Fm
Giddeahall
Upper Wraxall
Toplands Fm
Common Hill
Pew's Hill
The Shoe
Bury Camp
Cross Dyke
Slaughterford
Mill
Biddestone
Colerne Down
Hall Fm
Tumulus
Honeybrook Fm
Cemy
Lucknam Park
Colerne Park
Thickwood
Field Barn Fm
Bks
Wks
Mound
Euridge Manor Fm
Eastrip
Weavern Fm
Hartham Park
Airfield (dis)
Wr Twr
Colerne
Widdenham Fm
Upper Pickwick
Middle
Pickwick
Coll
Depot
Westwood Fm
Lid Brook
By Brook
Folly Fm
Half Way Firs
Corsh
Mill
Rudloe
Ditteridge
Alcombe
Cheney Court
Fogleigh Ho
Box Hill
Resr
Hawthorn
Hudswell
Box Tunnel
RAF Rudloe Manor
Westwells
Middlehill
Tunnel
Shockerwick Ho
Moor Green
Ashley
Box
Hazelbury Manor
HMS Royal Arthur
Chapel Plaister
Sheylors Fm
Tumuli
Henley
Wadswick
Fosse Way
ROMAN ROAD
A 420
B 3109
12
13
14
15
16
17
28
29

12 After 1 mile 1st R 'Mountain Bower'. At X-roads SA 'Nettleton, Castle Combe'

13 At 2nd X-roads SA 'Castle Combe'. At T-j sharply L downhill (NS)

14 Through Castle Combe up steady hill to T-j with B4039. R 'Chippenham'

15 After ¼ mile, on sharp LH bend, R (in effect SA) 'West Yatton, Giddeahall'

16 After 2 miles, at X-roads with the A420 by The Crown cross the grass verge SA to get to the lane opposite

17 At T-j R 'Corsham'. Through Biddestone past pubs. Ignore left turn on Chippenham Lane. Take next L after ¼ mile by a triangle of grass

18 At X-roads SA 'Lacock'

19 At next X-roads, with A4, SA 'Easton, Notton, Lacock, Melksham' – **take care**

20 Keep following signs for Lacock. 20 yards **before** T-j with A350 R (NS)

21 At T-j on Corsham Road L for 100 yards to A350

22 At T-j R then immediately L into Lacock, joining the Wiltshire Cycleway

23 50 yards past George Inn, on sharp LH bend, R (in effect SA) 'Melksham, Devizes, Trowbridge'

24 At small roundabout R then immediately R again along Folly Lane 'no through road'

25 **Take care** crossing busy A350. SA to continuation of Folly Lane 'Gastard'

26 After 2 miles at T-j by Harp and Crown PH R 'Corsham, Bath'

27 1st L at X-roads down Monks Lane. 'The Ridge' 'RN Store Depot Monks Park'

28 Follow road through Neston following signs for West Wells then Chapel Plaister

29 At large triangle of grass planted with trees just before main road bear L to T-j on B3109. L then immediately R (NS)

page 44

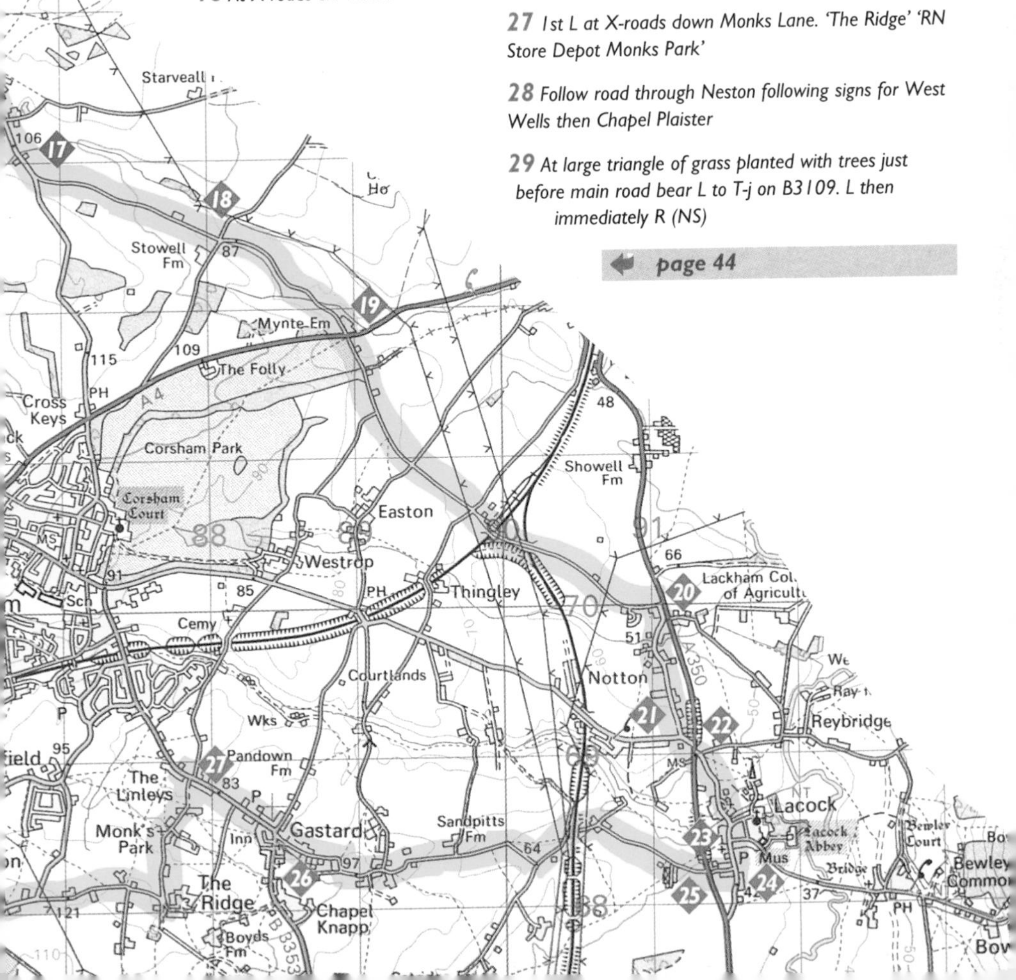

6 River valleys and canals near Marlborough

Starting from the attractive and prosperous town of Marlborough with its plethora of eating and drinking establishments, the ride heads southwest. It leaves the Kennet valley, crossing the ridge along which the old Wansdyke earthworks run, with fine views across the Vale of Pewsey into which it descends. The lovely village of Great Bedwyn with its most unusual post office, is the start of the second climb back into the Kennet valley at Ramsbury; from here the ride follows the river back to Marlborough.

Start

The High Street, Marlborough

P Follow signs in Marlborough

Distance and grade

36 miles

Easy

Terrain

Only two gentle climbs over the downs on a ride linking two river valleys

Nearest railway

Great Bedwyn (on the route itself)

Refreshments

Bruce Arms PH, **Easton Royal**
Cross Keys PH, **Great Bedwyn**
Bell Inn, **Ramsbury**
Royal Oak PH, **Wootton Rivers**
Plenty of choice in **Pewsey**
Plenty of choice in **Marlborough**
Seven Stars PH, **Woodborough**
Red Lion PH, **Axford**

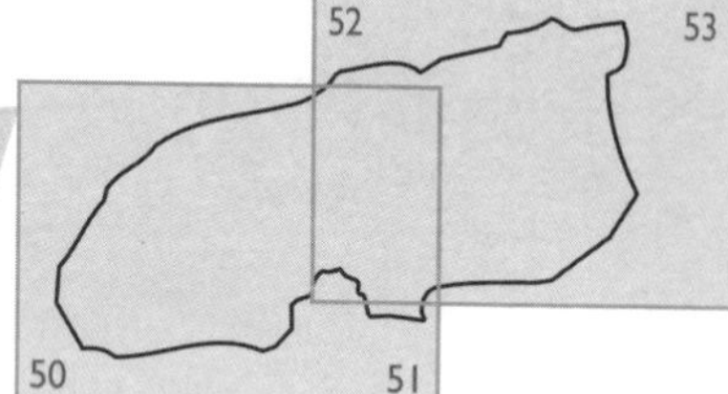

Marlborough

Lockeridge

Woodborough

Pewsey

Wootton Rivers

Places of interests

Marlborough *1*

Merlin, the magician of King Arthur's court, was, according to legend, buried under the town's castle mound. A noticeable feature of Marlborough is the Georgian High Street; one of the widest streets in the country, this was once one of the most important staging posts on the London to Bath road, now the A4. It is a reminder of the old town, much of which was destroyed or damaged by fires or the Civil War.

▲ *Marlborough*

Pewsey *7*

Famous for the White Horse, overlooking the town, that was cut in 1937 to commemorate the coronation of King George VI.

Ramsbury *21*

In Saxon times Ramsbury was the centre of a flourishing diocese with a cathedral and bishop but for nine centuries now it has been no more than a parish.

Crofton Great Bedwyn Ramsbury Axford

1 Take the A4 westwards out of Marlborough towards Calne and Chippenham

2 Go underneath red brick arch by school. After ¼ mile, opposite white railings on the right, just before 40 mph signs bear L onto a path by triangle of grass

3 Cross river, go past church and follow narrow tarmac lane. At T-j by triangle of grass opposite black and white thatched cottage L

4 After 2 miles, at T-j in Lockeridge L

5 Follow road for 6 miles, through Alton Barnes and Honey Street. Almost 2 miles after Alton Barnes and shortly after a 'Crossroads' sign 1st L opposite Smithy Lane 'Woodborough, Pewsey'

6 Follow signs for Pewsey. At X-roads SA

7 At T-j by church R. At T-j (with A345) at end of Wilcot Street R 'Upavon, Amesbury'

8 At mini-roundabout in Pewsey bear R past Royal Oak PH. After 300 yards L on B3087 'Burbage 4½'

9 At mini-roundabout SA 'Burbage'. SA through X-roads with No through Roads to right and left. Next L 'Milkhouse Water, Sunnyhill, West Wick'

10 Cross bridges over railway then stream and immediately R 'Wiltshire Cycleway'

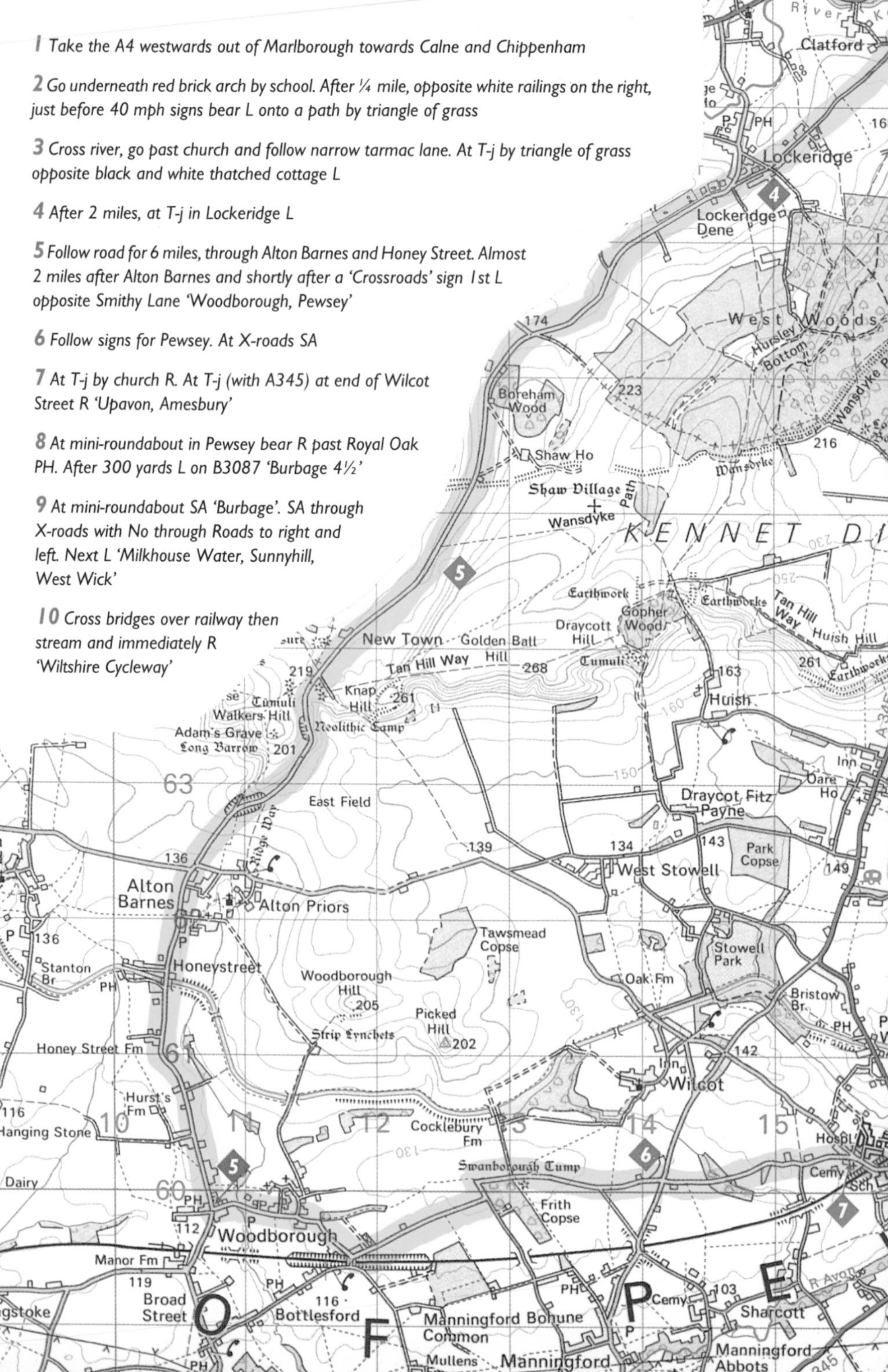

11 After ½ mile, at T-j L, then L again after 50 yards 'Wootton Rivers, Clench Common'

12 At T-j by Royal Oak PH in Wootton Rivers R 'Easton Royal, Milton Lilbourne'

13 Up and over two small hills. At T-j R 'Easton Royal'

14 At T-j with B3087 L 'Burbage 1'

15 After 1 mile, at offset X-roads 1st L 'Westcourt'

page 53

Downs
Mere Fm
Tumulus
Woodlands Fm
Sound Copse
Sound Bottom
Rabley Wood
154
195
Bay Br
Mildenhall Borders
House Fm
121
128
Thicket Copse
Axford
Axford Fm
Sluice
Marlborough Common
CH
Earthwork
Mildenhall
PH
129
119
Grove Fm
Sluice
Black Field
Stitchcombe
Coombe Fm
177
183
Sch
127
Coll
Earthworks
197
Hospl
MS
Forest Hill
Hens Wood
Earthwork
Posterne Hill
Forest Walk
Earthworks
Furze Coppice
East Croft Coppice
167
Puthall Fm
PC
193
Forest Walk
176
Grand Avenue
MS
Brown's Fm
147
Ashlade Firs
Little Frith
High Trees
dismtd rly
Braydon Hook
Luton Lye Cotts
Timbridge Fm
Crabtree Cotts
196
Eight Walks
Wansdyke
New Buildings
Great Lodge Fm
Savernake Lodge
ROMAN ROAD
SAVERNAKE
Cadley
dismtd rly
Tumuli
Tumulus
Birch Copse
158
Kingstones Fm
King Oak
Tumulus
Queen Oak
FOREST
147
Cotley's Fm
MS
The Warren
Park Fm
187
Leigh Hill
Column
St Katharine
157
166
189
Hat Gate Cottage
194
Column Ride
Tottenham
dismtd rlys
Terrace Hill
Durley
East Wick Fm
MS
Leigh Hill Copse
Apshill Copse
Tumuli
143
Burbage Wharf
195
185
Brimslade Fm
Ram Alley
Hotel
Deer Park
PH
Broomsgrove Wood
146
Wootton Rivers
Clench
A346
Kennet & Avon Canal
The Long Ho
173
MS
173
PH
Stibb Green
Cuckoo's Knob
Bowden Fm
Totteridge Fm
147
167
16
22
23

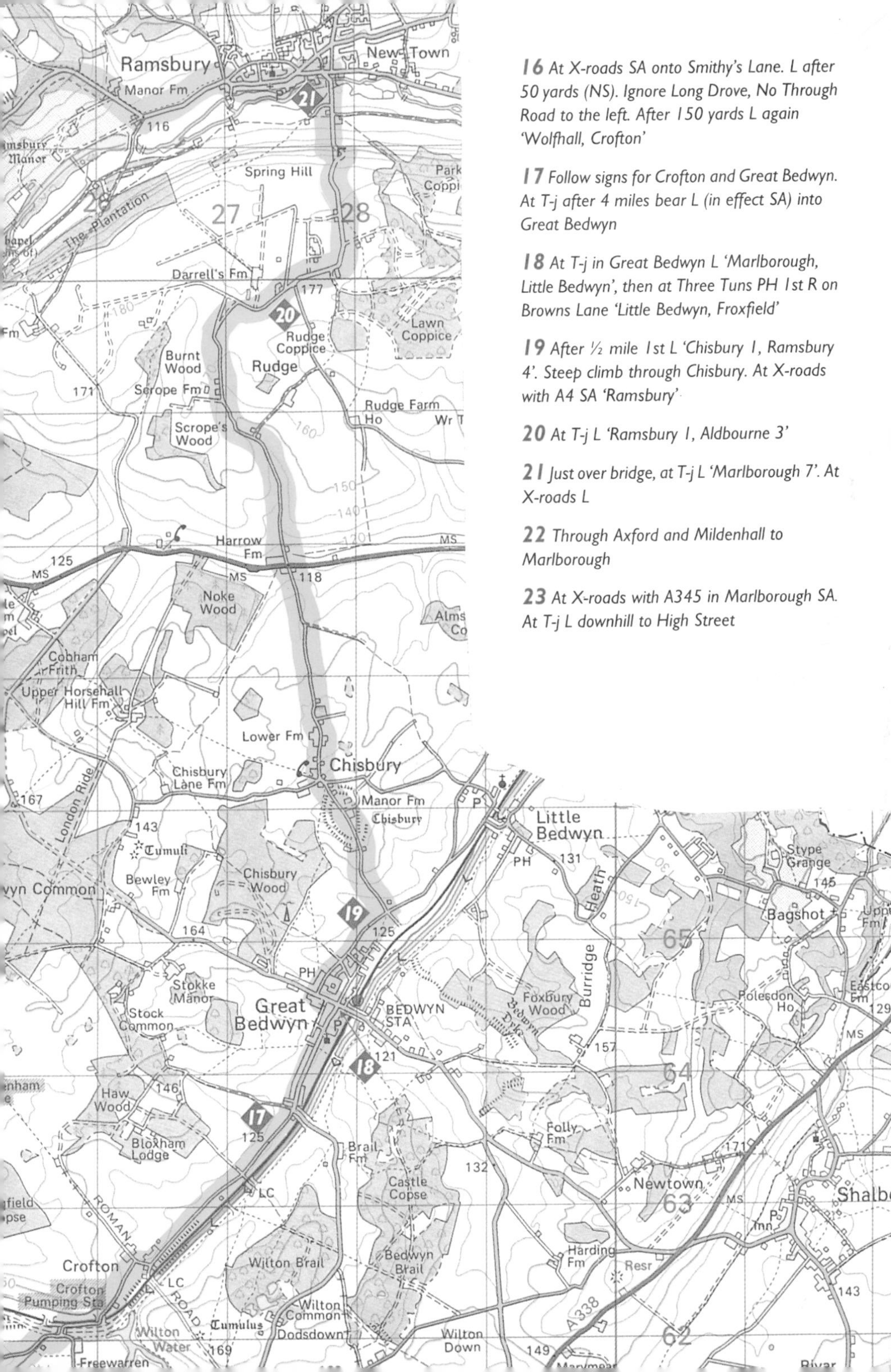

16 At X-roads SA onto Smithy's Lane. L after 50 yards (NS). Ignore Long Drove, No Through Road to the left. After 150 yards L again 'Wolfhall, Crofton'

17 Follow signs for Crofton and Great Bedwyn. At T-j after 4 miles bear L (in effect SA) into Great Bedwyn

18 At T-j in Great Bedwyn L 'Marlborough, Little Bedwyn', then at Three Tuns PH 1st R on Browns Lane 'Little Bedwyn, Froxfield'

19 After ½ mile 1st L 'Chisbury 1, Ramsbury 4'. Steep climb through Chisbury. At X-roads with A4 SA 'Ramsbury'

20 At T-j L 'Ramsbury 1, Aldbourne 3'

21 Just over bridge, at T-j L 'Marlborough 7'. At X-roads L

22 Through Axford and Mildenhall to Marlborough

23 At X-roads with A345 in Marlborough SA. At T-j L downhill to High Street

7 High on the Mendips

The Mendips are an outcrop of Carboniferous limestone stretching from Weston-super-Mare to Shepton Mallet, their most famous feature being the caves at Cheddar. The scenery is at times more reminiscent of the Yorkshire dales than southwest England, with squat grey stone houses and drystone walling.

The best views are to be found by making two detours from the main route, each of half a mile, to the radio masts near Charterhouse and to the edge of the steep southern slopes west of Priddy.

The ride skirts the steep hills of the western end of the range and climbs via Winscombe and Shipham to its highest point (870 feet) near Tynings Farm. It continues along the top of the ridge to Chewton Mendip, then brings you back via the towering cliffs of Cheddar Gorge, the tourist complex of Cheddar and the quieter pleasures of Axbridge.

Start

The Square, Axbridge

P Long-term parking in Meadow Street, Axbridge

Distance and grade

37 miles

Moderate/strenuous

Terrain

The Mendips are shaped like a whale's back. The ride climbs gently to the top and drops dramatically through the Cheddar Gorge

Nearest railway

Yatton, 6½ miles from Shipham

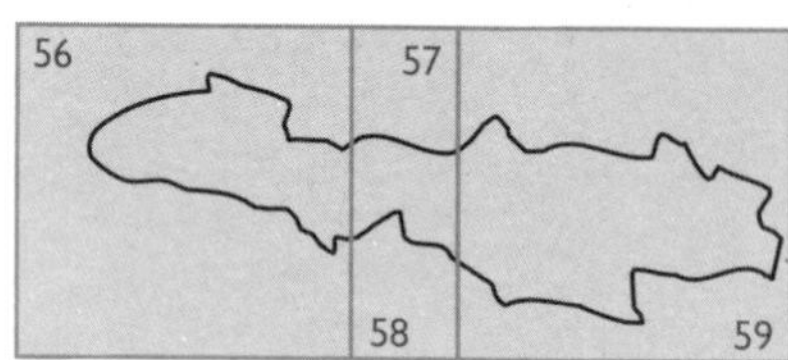

Axbridge Winscombe Star Shipham Charterhouse

Places of interest

King John's Hunting Lodge, Axbridge *2*
An early 15th-century merchant's timber-framed house that has been extensively restored and converted into a museum of local history and archaeology. It has no apparent connection with King John, or with hunting, but was used as an ale house in the 17th and 18th centuries.

Lillypool Cider and Cheese Farm, Shipham *11*
The farm dates back to the 18th century and houses an exhibition of farming equipment and cider mills. There is a café, children's play area and nature trail and local cider, cheese, homemade pickles and chutneys for sale.

Chewton Cheese Dairy, Priory Farm, Chewton Mendip *21*
One of the few dairies left making traditional Cheddar cheese from Fresian and Ayrshire herds. Morning coffee, farmhouse lunches and cream teas.

Cheddar Showcaves *29*
These spectacular caves within the limestone gorge are an attraction of outstanding natural beauty. There are magnificent crystalline formations that have taken over half a million years to form. The Cheddar Caves Museum displays various archeological finds.

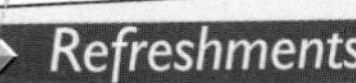

Refreshments

Lamb PH, plenty of choice in ***Axbridge***
Waldegrave Arms PH, ***East Harptree***
Hunters Lodge Inn, New Inn,
Queen Victoria Inn, ***Priddy***
Tea shop at Cheese Farm, ***Chewton Mendip***
Plenty of choice in ***Cheddar***
Waldegrave Arms PH, ***East Harptree***

Harptree Litton Chewton Mendip Priddy Cheddar

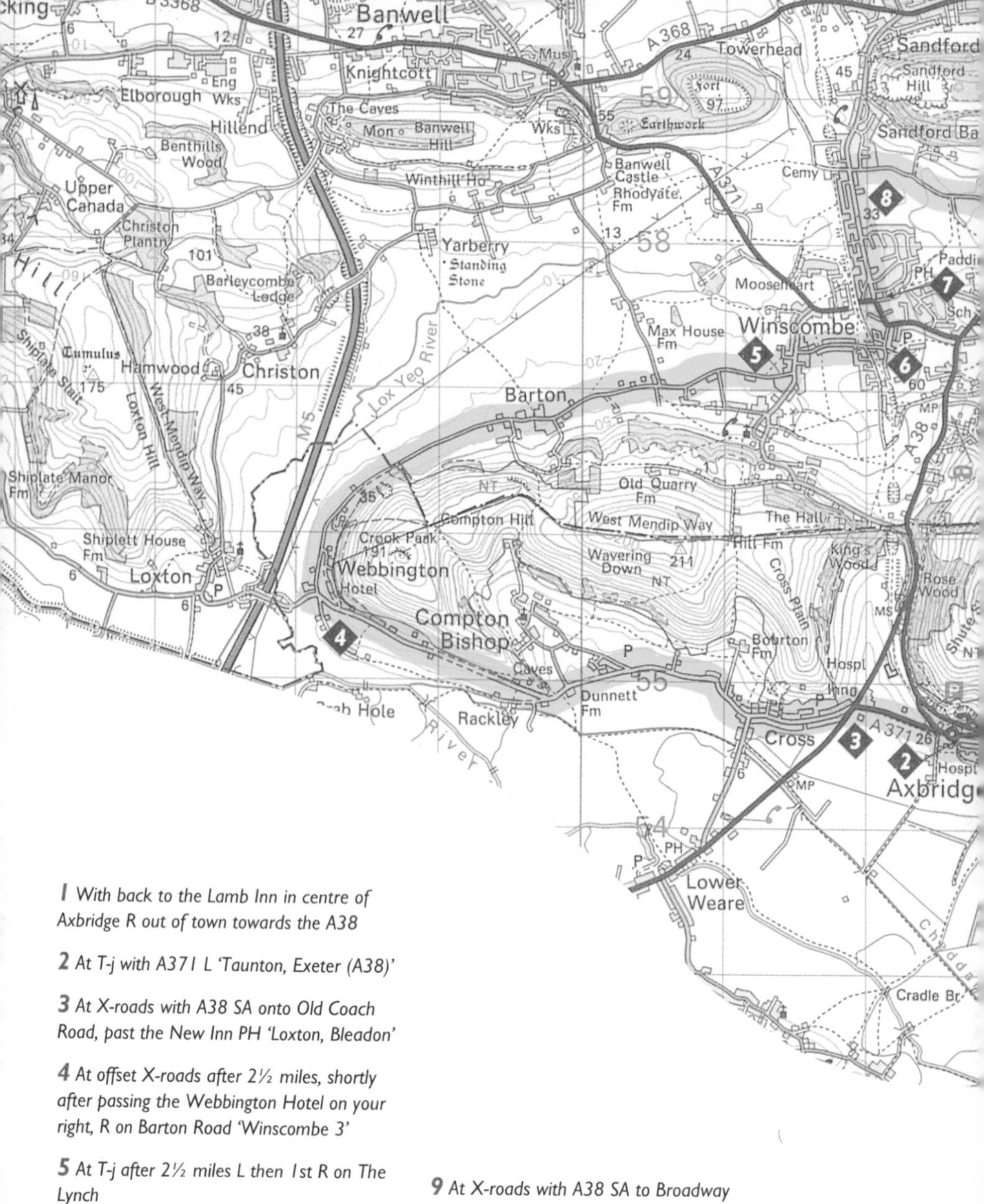

1 With back to the Lamb Inn in centre of Axbridge R out of town towards the A38

2 At T-j with A371 L 'Taunton, Exeter (A38)'

3 At X-roads with A38 SA onto Old Coach Road, past the New Inn PH 'Loxton, Bleadon'

4 At offset X-roads after 2½ miles, shortly after passing the Webbington Hotel on your right, R on Barton Road 'Winscombe 3'

5 At T-j after 2½ miles L then 1st R on The Lynch

6 At T-j with main road (Sidcot Lane) L (NS)

7 On sharp LH bend by the Woodborough PH bear R (in effect SA) on Sandford Road

8 Almost 1 mile after the Woodborough PH, shortly after passing the glazing company on right and dental surgery on left, as road flattens, 1st R on Shipham Lane (NS)

9 At X-roads with A38 SA to Broadway

*10 At X-roads in Shipham R 'Cheddar 3, Wells 11'. This road, which you follow for ¾ mile, may be busy, so **take care***

11 Shortly after the brow of the hill, just before Lillypool Cider Farm (good tea stop) L 'Charterhouse'

➡ ***page 58***

29 Through Cheddar Gorge and Cheddar. Opposite the Butchers Arms PH on your left R on Tweentown 'Weston-super-Mare' (A371)

30 After ½ mile, opposite the Catholic church, L on Lower North Street 'Baptist Church'

31 At T-j with A371, opposite shop, R then shortly L on Station Road, 'B3151 Wedmore'

32 2nd R, into Valley Line Industrial Estate, then on to Axbridge Cycleway

33 At end of cycleway, at T-j with main road L then L again 'Axbridge'

12 *Steady then steep climb to the plateau. After 3½ miles, L at X-roads 'Burrington 3½, Blagdon 2¼' (After 400 yards, 1st L to radio masts for fine views or on to trig point for even better ones!).* ***For short cut*** *turn R at the X-roads 'Priddy 3½, Cheddar 5½' and follow signs for Cheddar back to the start*

13 *At T-j with B3134 R 'Cheddar 7½'*

14 *After 1 mile, at truck repair yard L 'Compton Martin, West Harptree'*

15 *Go straight across two X-roads.* ***Take care*** *down steep hill!*

16 *At 3rd X-roads, with Mead Cottage ahead and a sign for 'Western Lane' near your right pedal (!), L*

17 *At the end of Middle Street, at T-j by the stores in East Harptree, R*

18 *After ¾ mile at T-j beneath telephone wires R (NS)*

19 *On sharp RH bend L 'Litton 1¼, Chewton Mendip 1'*

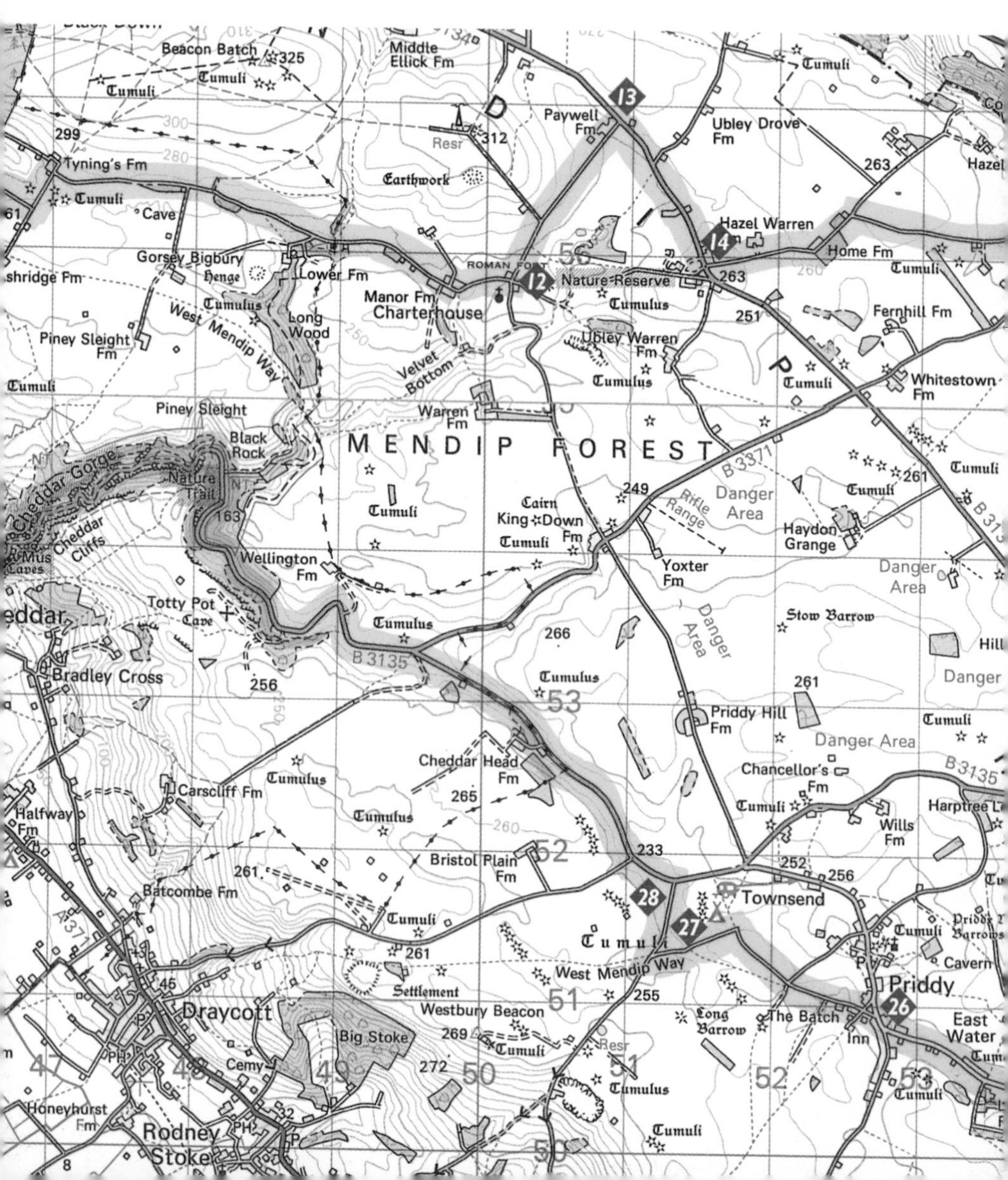

20 *At T-j with B3114 R 'Chewton Mendip ½, Wells 6¼'*

21 *At X-roads with A39 SA then 1st R on Bray's Batch, bearing L at fork. You are now on Puppy Lane*

22 *At X-roads R (NS). At X-roads with A39 SA 'Cheddar 9¾, Burrington 9½' (1st R to Priory Farm for an excellent tea stop)*

23 *At T-j with B3135 R 'Priddy, Cheddar, Burrington'*

24 *At X-roads by Miners Arms PH L 'Priddy, Milton'*

25 *At X-roads by Hunters Lodge Inn R 'Priddy 1½, Cheddar 7'*

26 *In Priddy L at New Inn PH*

27 *After 1 mile, at T-j R (NS) (detour L for ½ mile for fine views to the south)*

28 *At T-j with B3135 L 'Cheddar 5'*

page 57

8 The Somerset Levels south of Wedmore

Together with the Severn Vale, the Somerset Levels offer the flattest land covered by this book. However, flat does not mean boring, as the moors and levels are among the last remaining wetlands in the country and support a wide variety of wildlife. Huge mounds of rich dark peat and a network of drainage channels make this a most unusual landscape to cycle through. The ride also takes you through the mystical, magical town of Glastonbury, famous for its abbey and tor. As with all flat areas, very slight climbs can give fine viewpoints, and the climb onto the ridge southeast of Wedmore gives magnificent views not only of the Levels but also of the Mendips to the north.

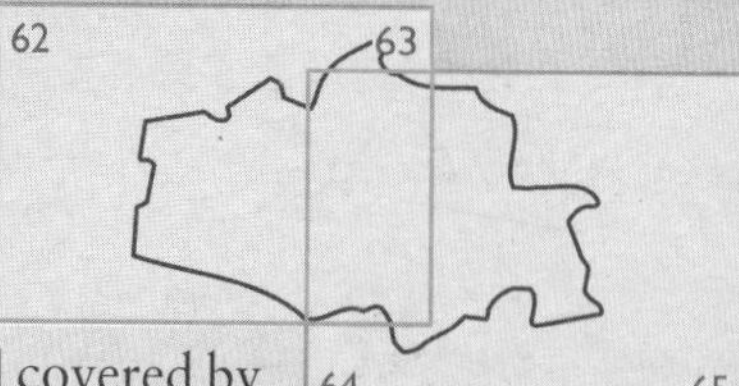

Start

The car park in Wedmore

P As above

Distance and grade

32 miles

Easy

Terrain

Flat, except for one climb on to the ridge southeast of Wedmore

Nearest railway

Highbridge, 4 miles from Huntspill Moor

Background picture: Glastonbury and Glastonbury Tor

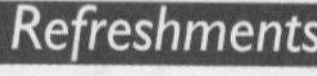

Refreshments

George PH, *plenty of choice in* **Wedmore**
King William PH, **Catcott**
Ashcott Inn, **Ashcott**
Plenty of choice in **Glastonbury**
Panborough PH, **Panborough**

Wedmore Cossington Catcott Shapwick

Places of interest

The Peat Moors Visitor Centre

Situated at the Willows Garden Centre, a 2 mile detour left at Shapwick crossroads (instruction 7). The centre illustrates the life, history, archaeology and natural history of the Somerset Levels. Tea rooms are also located at the garden centre.

Glastonbury 11

The ruined abbey at Glastonbury is on the site of the earliest Christian church of England and the body of King Arthur is reputed to be buried beneath the high altar. The ruins today consist mainly of the abbey church, St Mary's Chapel and various monastic buildings. In the gatehouse there is a model of the abbey as it was in 1539. The Tor dominating the town in the east provides spectacular views and is crowned by the remaining tower of 15th-century St Michael's Chapel.

Somerset Rural Life Museum, Glastonbury 11

Set in what was once the principal tithe barn of the abbey, it has a late Victorian farmhouse, an exhibition of Cheddar cheese making and other displays of agriculture and Somerset industries. Various outdoor demonstrations and activities are held in the courtyard.

1 Out of Wedmore on the B3139 towards Burnham. After ½ mile, at the edge of Wedmore, just past Wedmore First School on the right next L (NS)

2 Through Heath House down onto moor. At T-j with broad stone track ahead R (NS)

3 After 1½ miles 1st L between rows of pollarded willow trees (NS). After ½ mile 1st L

4 After 1¼ miles, L at T-j 'Edington, Bridgwater', then 1st R 'Huntspill, Bridgwater'

5 At sharp RH bend L 'Gold Corner ¾, Cossington 3'

6 At T-j in Cossington L on Middle Road. Follow for 3½ miles through Chilton Polden, bypassing Catcott, turning L at X-roads 1¼ miles past Catcott on Church Lane 'Shapwick ½, Westhay 3½'

7 At X-roads in Shapwick, SA onto Northbrook Road 'Ashcott 1½, Glastonbury 6¾'. After almost ½ mile just before '7.5 Ton Weight Limit' sign 1st R

page 65

17 1st R in Sand 'Wedmore ¾, Cheddar 4¾'. At T-j R 'Shapwick, Glastonbury'. At mini-roundabout SA onto Grants Lane to return to start

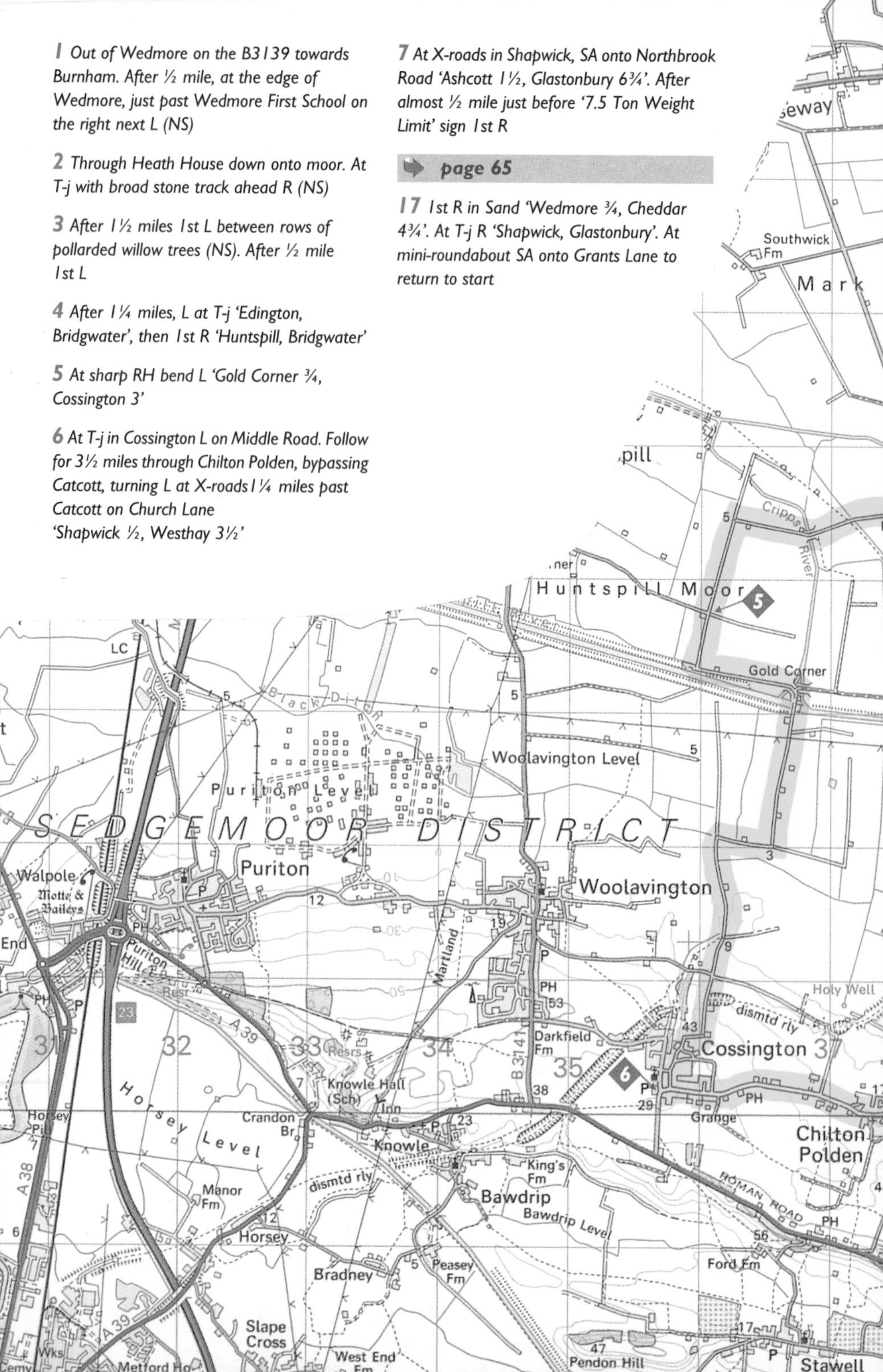

Mark
Blackford
Wedmore
Pool Bridge Fm
Totney Fm
Yarrow
Westham
Sand
Latcham
Stook Ho
Lands End Fm
Heath House
Hall
Mudgley Hill
Tealham Moor
Aller Moor
North Drain
River House Fm
Brue
River Bridge
Blakeway Fm
Tadham Moor
Fir Tree Fm
Hurst Fm
Burtle Hill
Catcott Grounds
dismantled railway
Burtle
Westhay Level
Peacock Fm
Westhay Br
South Drain
Honeygar Fm
Westhay
Catcott Br
Edington Heath
Westhay Heath
Catcott Heath
The Willows
Heath View Fm
Edington Moor
Nidons
Canada Fm
Shapwick Heath
Meare Heath
Moorgate Fm
Edington
Holy Well
Catcott
Langlands Fm
Kent Fm
Moat
Shapwick Ho (Hotel)
Northbrook Fm
Ashcott
Manor Fm
Shapwick
Fifteen Acre Copse
Beerway Fm
B 3139
B 3151
A 39

Heath House
Mudgley Hill
Mudgley
Bagley
New Town
Panborough
Aller Moor
North Drain
Blakeway Fm
Tadham Moor
Fir Tree Fm
B3151
Westhay Moor
Rosebud Fm
Brook Fm
Godney
Westhay Level
Peacock Fm
Westhay Br
Honeygar Fm
Westhay
Decoy Rhyne
Lower Godney
Meare Pool
Manor Fm
Oxenpill
Meare Fm
Abbot's Fish Ho
Westhay Heath
The Willows
Heath View Fm
Cemy
Meare
Wr Twr
Stileway
Canada Fm
Meare Heath
Shapwick Heath
Peat Wks
Rice Fm
White Bridge
Little Ranch
43
44
45
46
47
Moorgate Fm
Ashcott Corner
Glastonbury Heath
Fishpond Fm
Street Heath
Ashcott Heath
Walton Heath
dismtd rly
Kent Fm
Moat
Northbrook Fm
Shapwick Ho (Hotel)
Fifteen Acre Copse
Buscott
Cradlebridge Fm
Shapwick
Avalon Fm
Beerway Fm
Millslade Fm
Park End Fm
Sharpham Park
Ashcott
Inn
Pedwell
Whitley Fm
Asney
Portland
Factory
Lockhill Hall
A 361
Greinton
Berhill
Walton

7 At X-roads in Shapwick, SA onto Northbrook Road 'Ashcott 1½, Glastonbury 6¾'. After almost ½ mile just before '7.5 Ton Weight Limit' sign 1st R

8 Bear L at fork into Ashcott. At T-j at the end of Chestnut Lane L. After 300 yards, just before '7.5 ton weight limit' signs for Ridgeway and Station Road bear diagonally R

9 After ½ mile 1st L (NS) then at T-j after ¾ mile L (NS)

10 At T-j by Avalon Farm L. At next T-j R 'Glastonbury, Street', then 1st L over bridge with iron railings into Glastonbury

11 After exploring Glastonbury, from the Market Place take the B3151 (Northload Road) towards Meare

12 ½ mile from centre of Glastonbury, just before bridge, R 'Godney 2' past Glastonbury Football Club ground

13 At X-roads L 'Lower Godney 1¼'

14 Follow road around sharp RH bend soon after pub and follow signs for Wedmore. At T-j with B3139 L 'Wedmore 3½, Burnham 12¼'

15 Climb through Panborough. Shortly after brow of hill, at start of village of Theale turn L 'Bagley ¾, Mudgley 1½'

16 At X-roads SA 'Sand, Blackford'

page 62

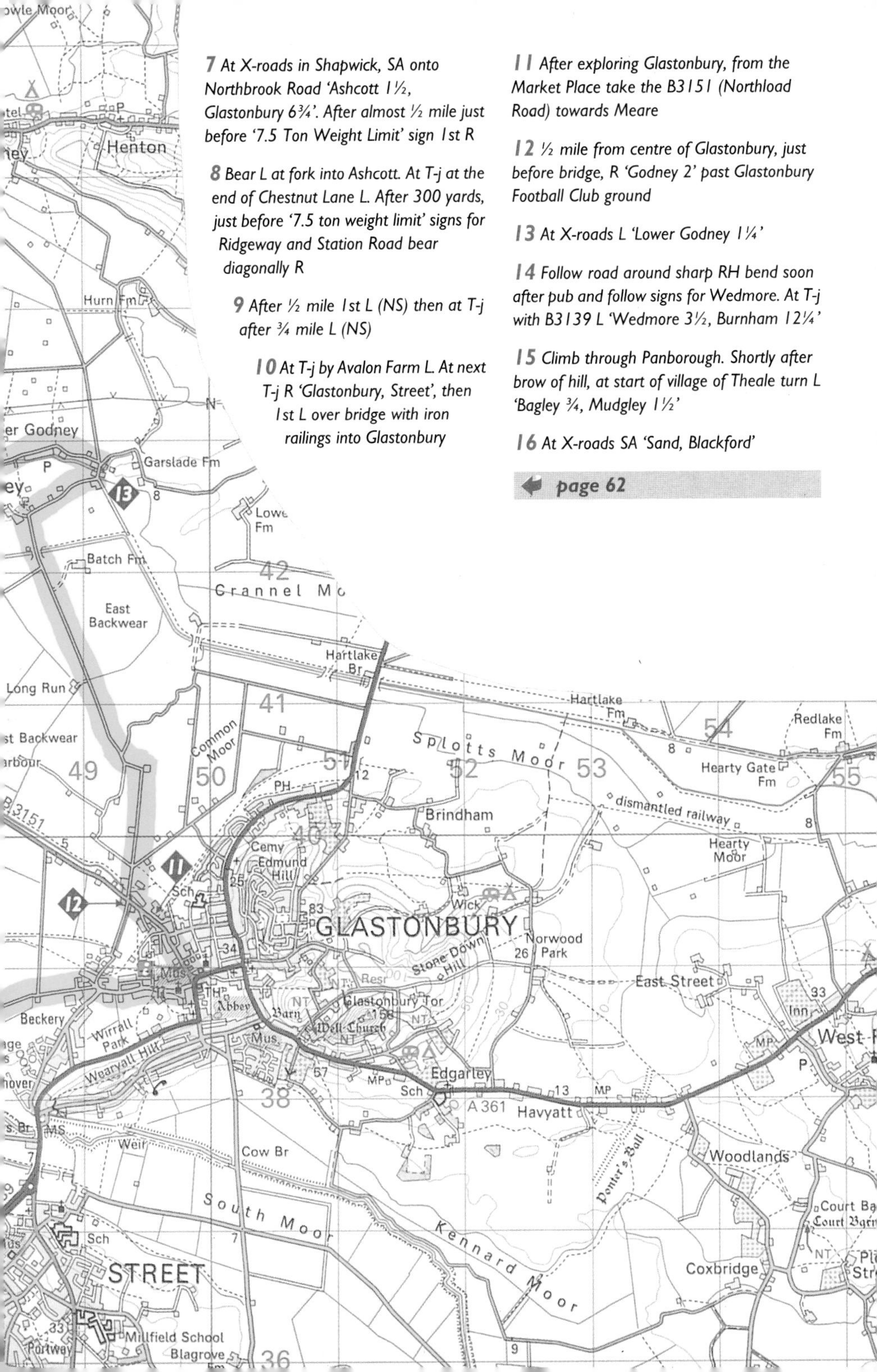

The roof of Exmoor, west of Dulverton

Dulverton is a beautiful place set in the valley of the Barle but if you like cycling away from main roads, there are no real alternatives to some very steep climbs. The climb onto the moor is probably the hardest in the whole book so don't feel disheartened if you have to walk; it is only a mile and gives you access to a magnificent ridge ride on the very roof of Exmoor.

70 71 68 69

The Sportsman's Inn at Sandyway Cross is about as unlikely a location for a pub as you will ever find and a welcome stopping-off point before the second major climb (much more gradual this time, 300 feet in 2 miles) up to the high point of the ride (1600 feet) near Kinsford Gate.

It is time to strap everything down and make doubly sure your brakes work for the descent into Simonsbath and a choice of refreshment stops. The final climb is to the top of Winsford Hill and the long descent through woodland by the River Barle to return to Dulverton.

Start

The Lion Hotel, Dulverton

P Follow signs in centre of Dulverton

Distance and grade

32 miles

Strenuous

Terrain

1150-feet climb from Dulverton to the highpoint at Hangley Cleave divided into three sections: very steep 550-feet climb out of Dulverton, gentle 300-feet climb across Anstey and Molland Common, steady 300-feet climb from Sportsman's Inn to the top. 330-feet climb out of Simonsbath. 230-feet climb from Comer's Cross to Winsford Hill

Nearest railway

Tiverton Parkway, 18 miles from Dulverton

Dulverton

Molland Common

Kinsford G

Places of interest

Dulverton

Named 'The Secret Place' by Saxon settlers Dulverton has a special unspoilt charm with narrow lanes and cobbled alleys. The Guildhall Centre in the middle of Dulverton has exhibitions of all kinds throughout the year. At Exmoor House beside the River Barle there are the headquarters of the National Park Authority and Dulverton Art Gallery.

Refreshments

Plenty of choice in
Dulverton
Sportsman's Inn,
Sandyway Cross
Simonsbath Hotel,
Simonsbath

▲ *Exmoor*

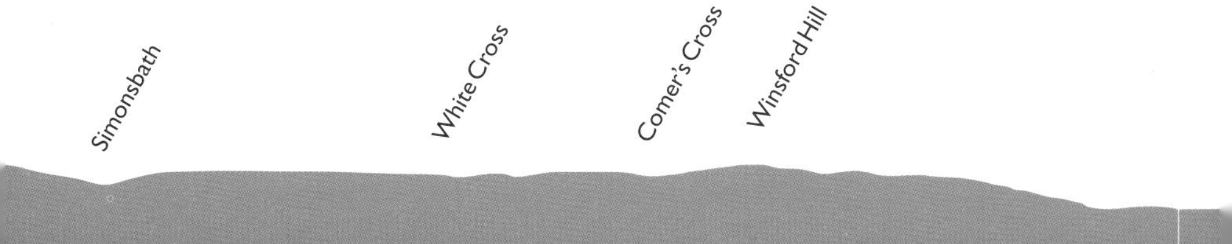

Simonsbath
White Cross
Comer's Cross
Winsford Hill

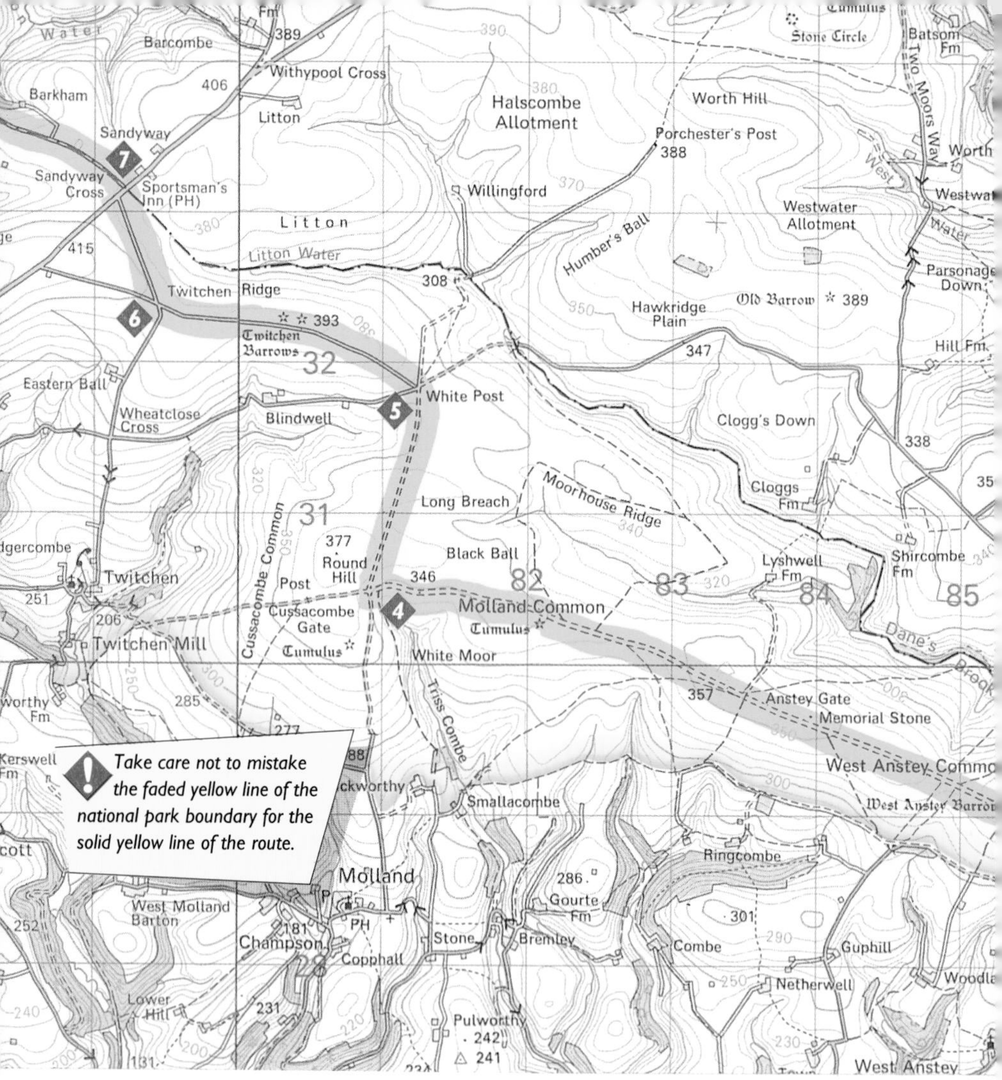

1 Take the B3223 towards Lynton

2 After 1 mile L 'Hawkridge 4'. 1st climb (500 feet)

3 At Five Ways Cross SA 'Molland 6'

4 After 5 miles along this magnificent ridge, at X-roads at Ridgeway Cross R 'Hawkridge 4, Withypool 6'

5 After 1 mile at White Post Cross L over cattle grid and immediately bear R uphill

6 *At Mudgate Cross R 'Sandyway, Withypool'*

7 *At Sandyway Cross R then L, following signs for Simonsbath or stop at the pub here*

page 70

13 *4th climb (230 feet) to Winsford Hill*

14 *Final descent (465 feet) to Dulverton*

8 *2nd climb (300 feet) to highest point of ride*

9 *At Kinsford Gate Cross R 'Simonsbath, Lynton'*

10 *Steep drop to Simonsbath and choice of restaurant or pub*

11 *At T-j in Simonsbath R on B3223 'Exford, Minehead', – 3rd climb (230 feet)*

12 *This section may be busy. After 5 miles R on B3223 'Withypool 2½, Dulverton 10'*

13 *4th climb (230 feet) to Winsford Hill*

 **page 69**

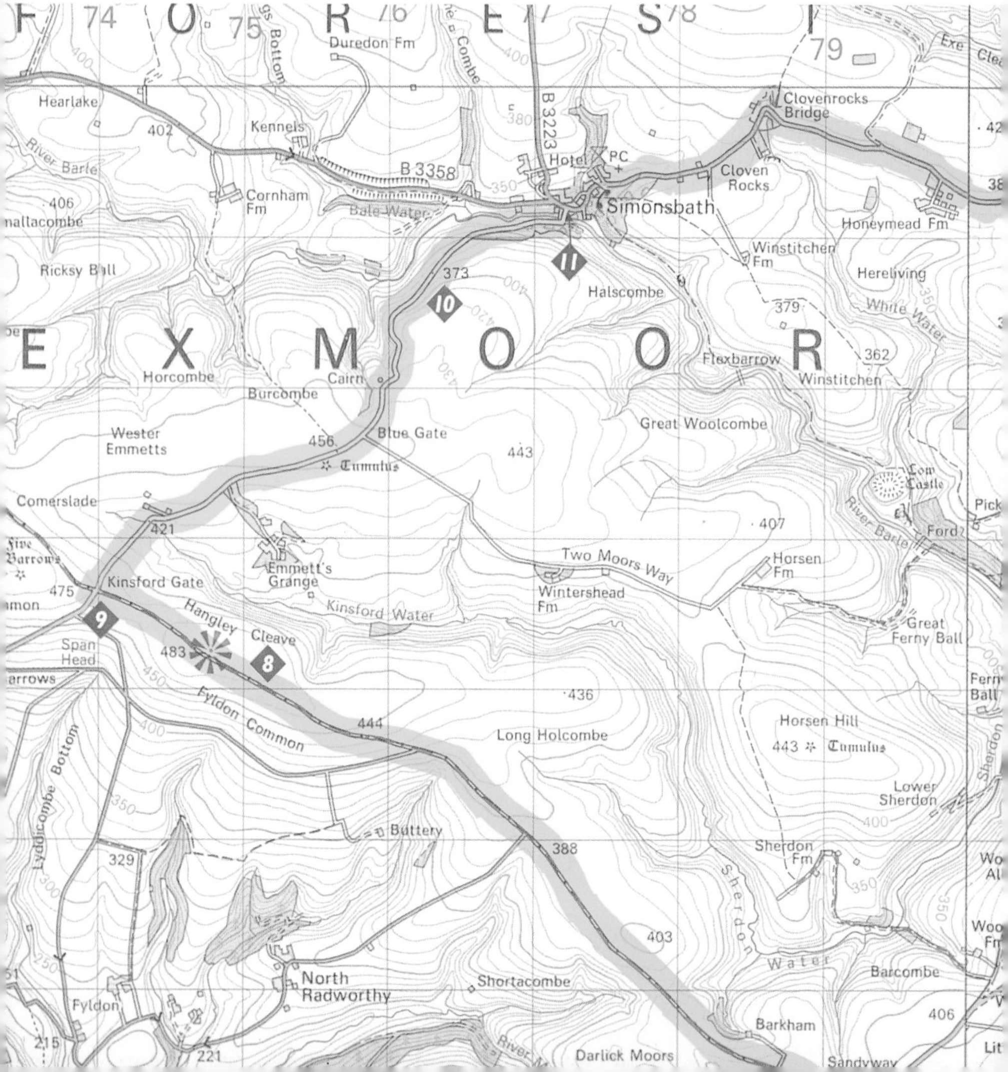

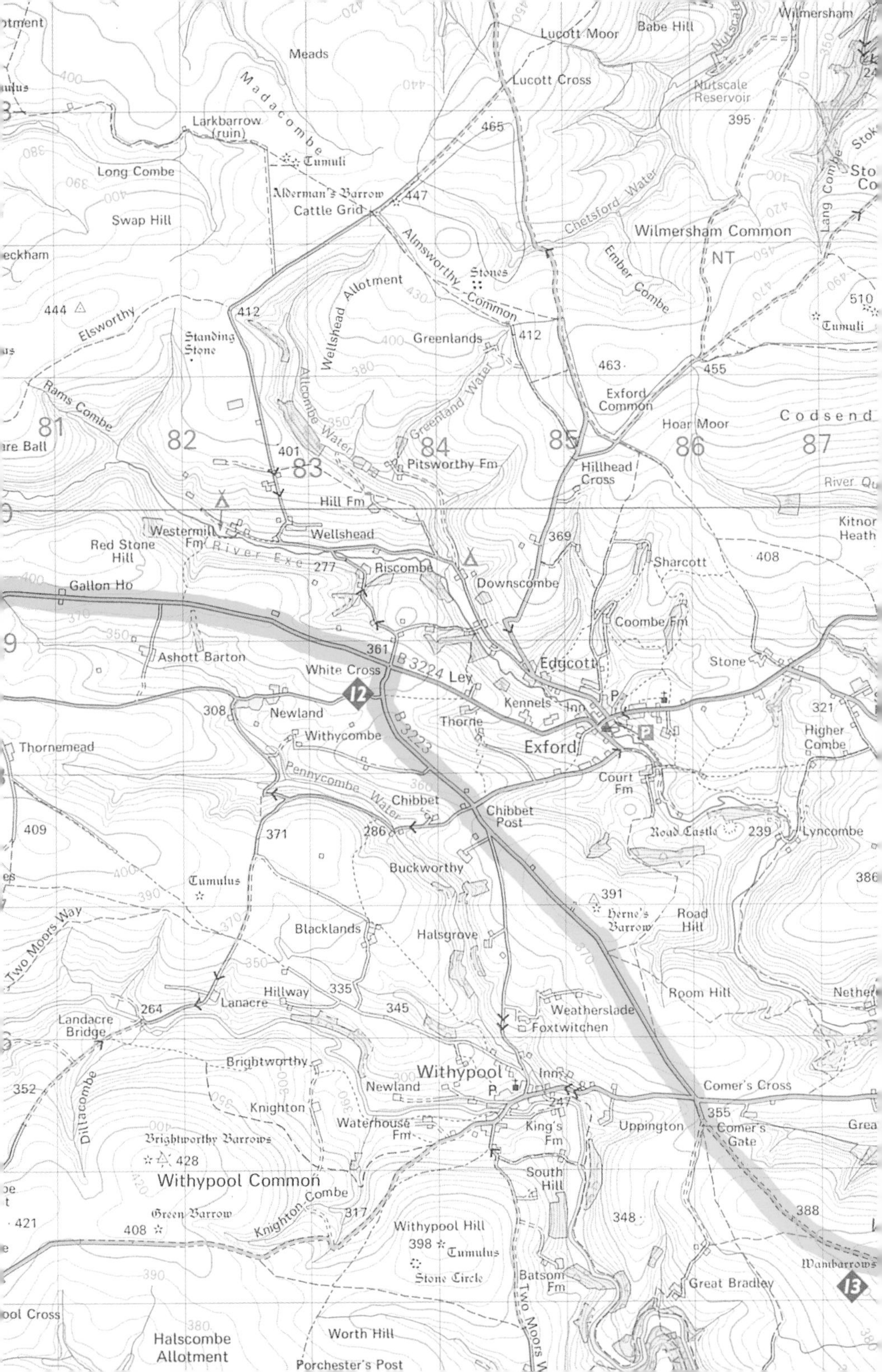

Lucott Moor
Babe Hill
Wilmersham
Meads
Madacombe
Lucott Cross
Nutscale Reservoir
395
Larkbarrow (ruin)
465
Tumuli
Long Combe
Alderman's Barrow
447
Cattle Grid
Swap Hill
Chetsford Water
Wilmersham Common
Almsworthy Common
NT
Ember Combe
Stones
Wellshead Allotment
444
Elsworthy
412
Greenlands
412
510
Tumuli
Standing Stone
463
455
Rams Combe
Allcombe Water
Greenland Water
Exford Common
Codsend
Hoar Moor
81
82
83
84
85
86
87
401
Pitsworthy Fm
Hillhead Cross
River Quarme
Hill Fm
Westermill Fm
Wellshead
Kitnor Heath
Red Stone Hill
River Exe
277
Riscombe
369
Sharcott
408
Gallon Ho
Downscombe
Coombe Fm
Ashott Barton
361
Edgcott
Stone
White Cross
B 3224
Ley
12
Kennels
Inn
321
308
Newland
Thorne
Higher Combe
Thornemead
Withycombe
Exford
B 3223
Pennycombe Water
Chibbet
Court Fm
Chibbet Post
409
371
286
Road Castle
239
Lyncombe
Buckworthy
386
Tumulus
391
Herne's Barrow
Road Hill
Two Moors Way
Blacklands
Halsgrove
Room Hill
Hillway
335
345
Lanacre
264
Weatherslade
Landacre Bridge
Foxtwitchen
Brightworthy
Withypool
Inn
Comer's Cross
352
Newland
247
Knighton
Waterhouse Fm
King's Fm
355
Uppington
Comer's Gate
Dillacombe
Brightworthy Barrows
428
South Hill
Withypool Common
Knighton Combe
421
Green Barrow
317
408
Withypool Hill
348
388
398
Tumulus
Stone Circle
Wambarrows
Batsom Fm
Great Bradley
13
Halscombe Allotment
Worth Hill
Porchester's Post

Over the Brendon Hills, east of Dulverton

The two major climbs in this ride are well worth the effort for the superb views from the Brendon Hills. The first climb starts at the ford at Bury, east of Dulverton, and swiftly reaches the top of Haddon Hill, where the view opens out. More gentle climbing takes you to the first high point of 1300 feet at the masts near Brendon Hill Farm. A 4-mile descent, which provides occasional views of the sea, drops you at the Washford River in Hungerford. From here a lovely riverside climb (1150 feet) brings you onto the second 1300-foot high point. An undulating ridge ride drops steeply at the end to return to Dulverton.

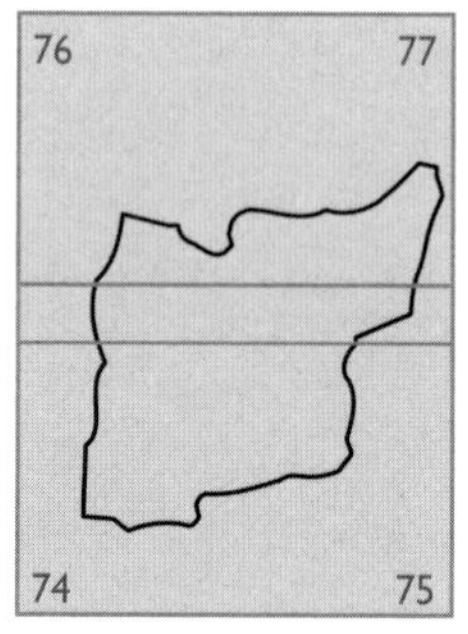

Start

The Lion Hotel, Dulverton

P Follow signs in Dulverton

Distance and grade

34 miles

Strenuous

Terrain

Steep 630-feet climb from Bury onto Haddon Hill. 530-feet climb from Upton to the masts at the top of the hill. 1200-feet climb over 9 miles from Washford to Lype Hill

Nearest railway

Washford, 1 mile from Hungerford

Refreshments

Plenty of choice in **Dulverton**
Ralegh's Cross Inn, **Ralegh's Cross**
Royal Oak PH, **Luxborough**
Valiant Soldier PH, **Roadwater**

Dulverton
Bury
Haddon Hill
Upton
Sticklepath
Hun

▲ *Exmoor*

Places of interest

West Somerset Railway

This is Britain's longest independent railway. It runs from Bishop's Lydeard near Taunton to Minehead passing about half a mile from the route at Washford. Many of the trains are steam-hauled.

Cleeve Abbey, Washford 7

Cleeve Abbey was founded by the Earl of Lincoln in 1198 and is the only Cistercian abbey in Somerset. It has been well renovated and the remaining buidings include the refectory, chapter house, common-room and the cloisters.

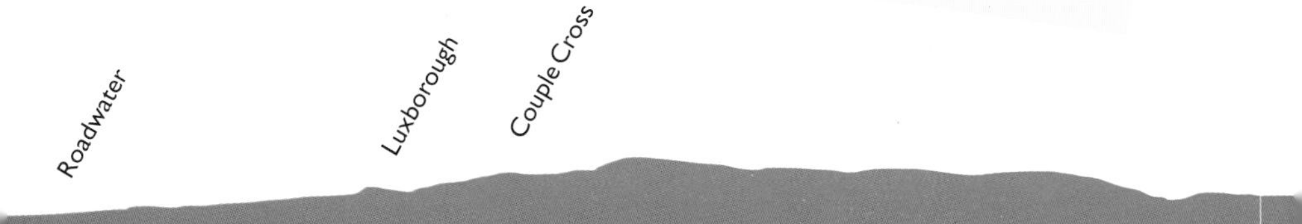

Roadwater

Luxborough

Couple Cross

Coppleham
Armoor
Kendle Fm
Ford Fm
Blagdon Fm
Leigh Fm
Exton
Week
Bridgetown
Inn
Combeshead Fm
King's Brompton Fm
Blagdon Hill
Howetown Fm
Hone
Hollam Fm
Miltons
Pulham River
Kings Brompton Forest
Higher Foxhanger Fm
Shircombe
Nature Trail
Brompton Regis
Woolcotts
Broford Fm
Kents Fm
Weir
Weatherham Fm
Daws Fm
Hill Fm
Higher Cowlings
Holworthy
Chilly Bridge
Oatway
Redcross Fm
Storridge Hill
Wimbleball Lake
Halscombe Fm
Vean
Harewood Fm
Lyncombe Fm
Stockham
Court Down
Oxgrove
South Greenslade Fm
West Hill Wood
Upton Fm
Hartford Bottom
Hartford
River Haddeo
Northcombe
Quarry (dis)
Baronsdown
Barlynch Fm
Barlynch Wood
Hadborough
Loursa Gate
Clammer
Hollam
Bury Hill
Haddon Fm
Dulverton
Hele Br
B 3222
A 396
Chapple Fm
Frogwell Fm
South Haddon
Surridge Fm
Inn
Cemy
Ford
Bury
Bury Castle
Leigh Barton
Withywine
Pixton Park
Beasley Fm
Combe
Allers Wood
Weir Ho
Pixton Hill
Pixy Copse
Combeland
B 3190
Brockhole
Brushford
Perry Fm
Warmore
Willishayes Fm
Hayne Fm
Timewell
Morebath Manor
Coombe
Hotel
Langaller Fm
dismtd rly
Burston
Court
Kents Hill
Hulverton Hill
Croft Fm
Riphay Barton
Poole Fm
Wks
Fishery
Ashtown Fm
Morebath
Loyterr
Rocks
Exebridge
Keens
Westwd
Wilsons Fm
Moore Fm

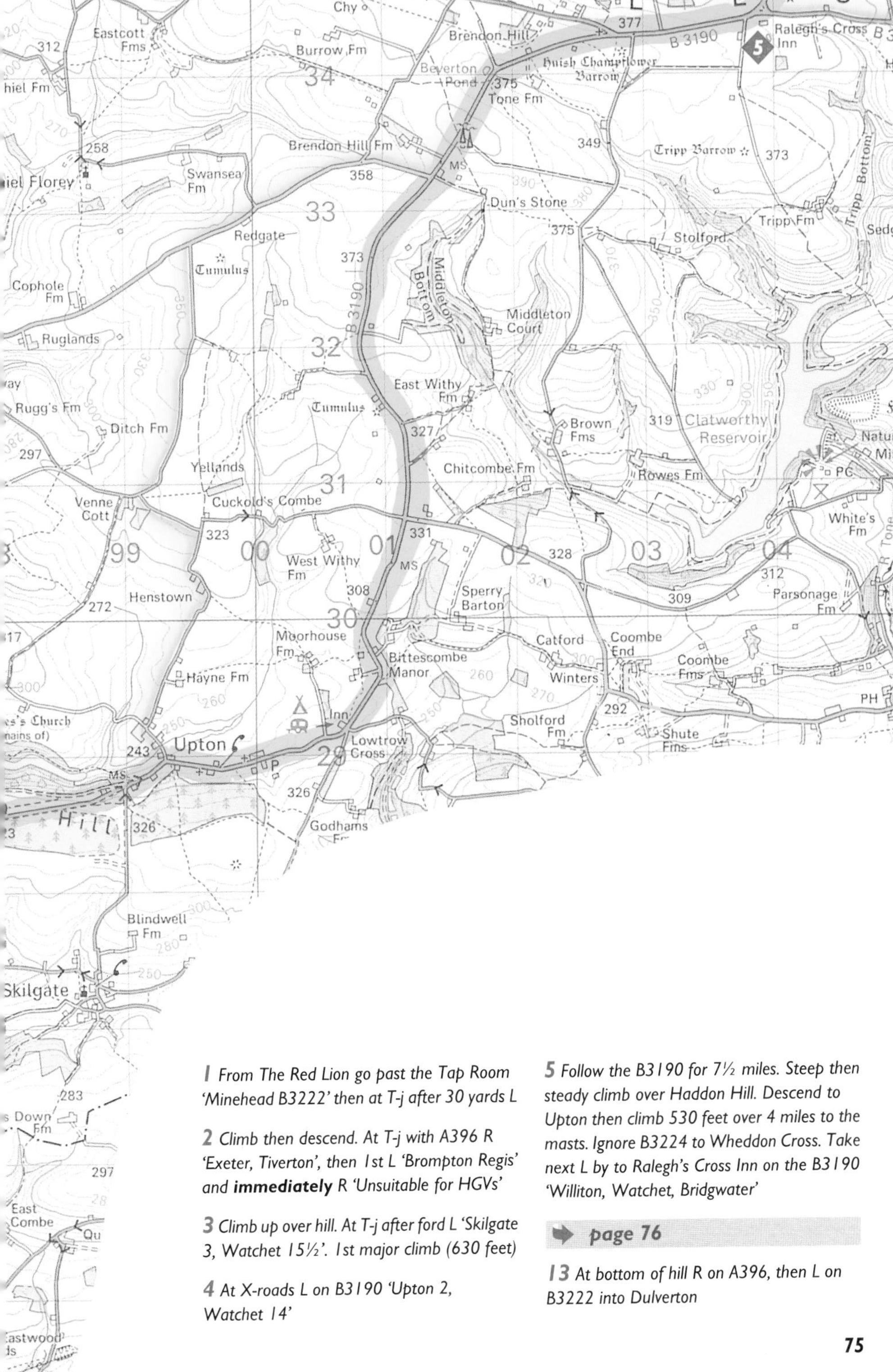

1 *From The Red Lion go past the Tap Room 'Minehead B3222' then at T-j after 30 yards L*

2 *Climb then descend. At T-j with A396 R 'Exeter, Tiverton', then 1st L 'Brompton Regis' and **immediately** R 'Unsuitable for HGVs'*

3 *Climb up over hill. At T-j after ford L 'Skilgate 3, Watchet 15½'. 1st major climb (630 feet)*

4 *At X-roads L on B3190 'Upton 2, Watchet 14'*

5 *Follow the B3190 for 7½ miles. Steep then steady climb over Haddon Hill. Descend to Upton then climb 530 feet over 4 miles to the masts. Ignore B3224 to Wheddon Cross. Take next L by to Ralegh's Cross Inn on the B3190 'Williton, Watchet, Bridgwater'*

➡ page 76

13 *At bottom of hill R on A396, then L on B3222 into Dulverton*

5 Follow the B3190 for 7½ miles. Steep then steady climb over Haddon Hill. Descend to Upton then climb 530 feet over 4 miles to the masts. Ignore B3224 to Wheddon Cross. Take next L by to Ralegh's Cross Inn on the B3190 'Williton, Watchet, Bridgwater'

6 Fast descent, short climb, 2nd fast descent. At X-roads after almost 4 miles by large red sandstone house and signpost with myriad Somerset names L 'Washford 1¾, Minehead 7¾'

7 At White Horse Inn in Hungerford L 'Roadwater 1½, Treborough 3½, Luxborough 5¾'. Start of 2nd climb (1200 feet over 9 miles)

8 At the far end of Roadwater, 400 yards after the Valiant Soldier PH R 'Luxborough 3¾'

9 In Luxborough ignore 1st R near Inn but take 2nd R, after crossing bridge 'Dunster 5½'

10 Steep climb to Churchtown. At T-j by Butchers Farm bear L (in effect SA) then after further ½ mile climb by triangle of grass with trees and bench L 'Timberscombe 3¾, Wheddon Cross 4½'

11 At X-roads L 'Wheddon Cross 3, Dulverton 9'

12 At X-roads SA 'Brompton Regis 4¼, Dulverton 7½'

page 75

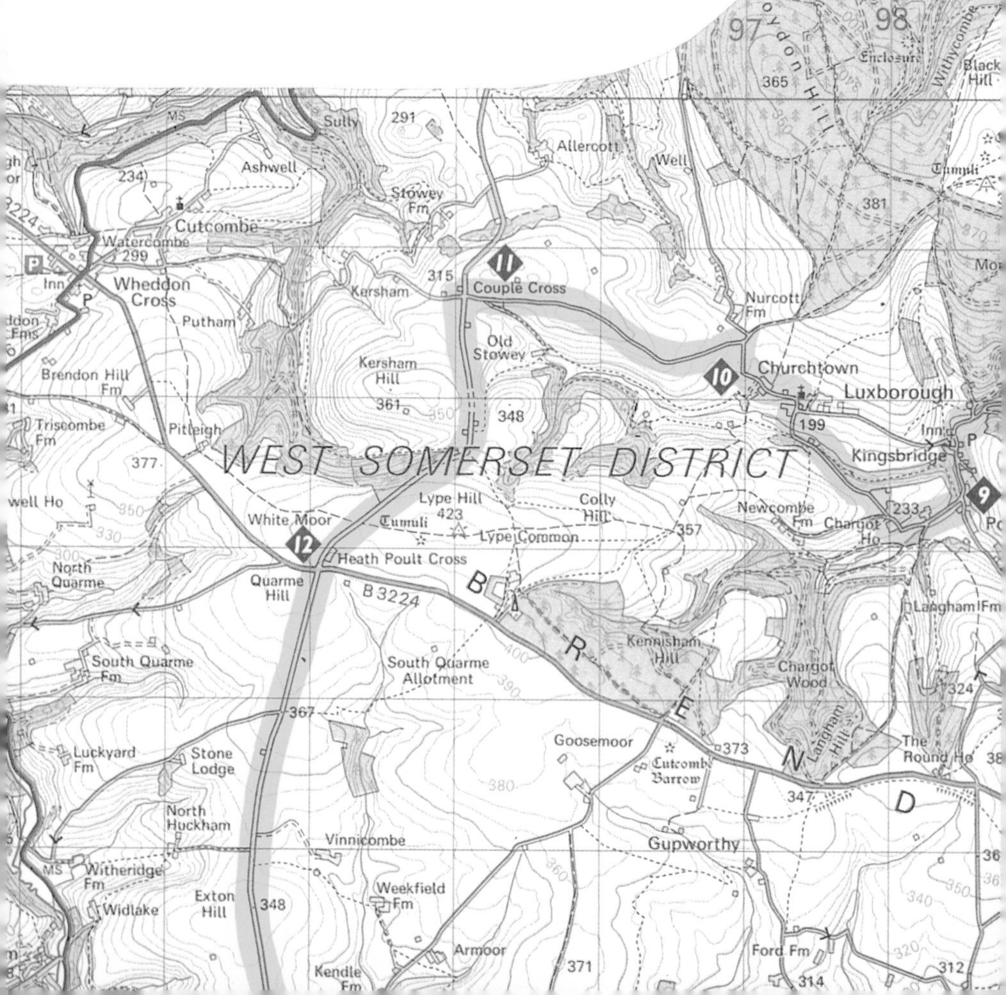

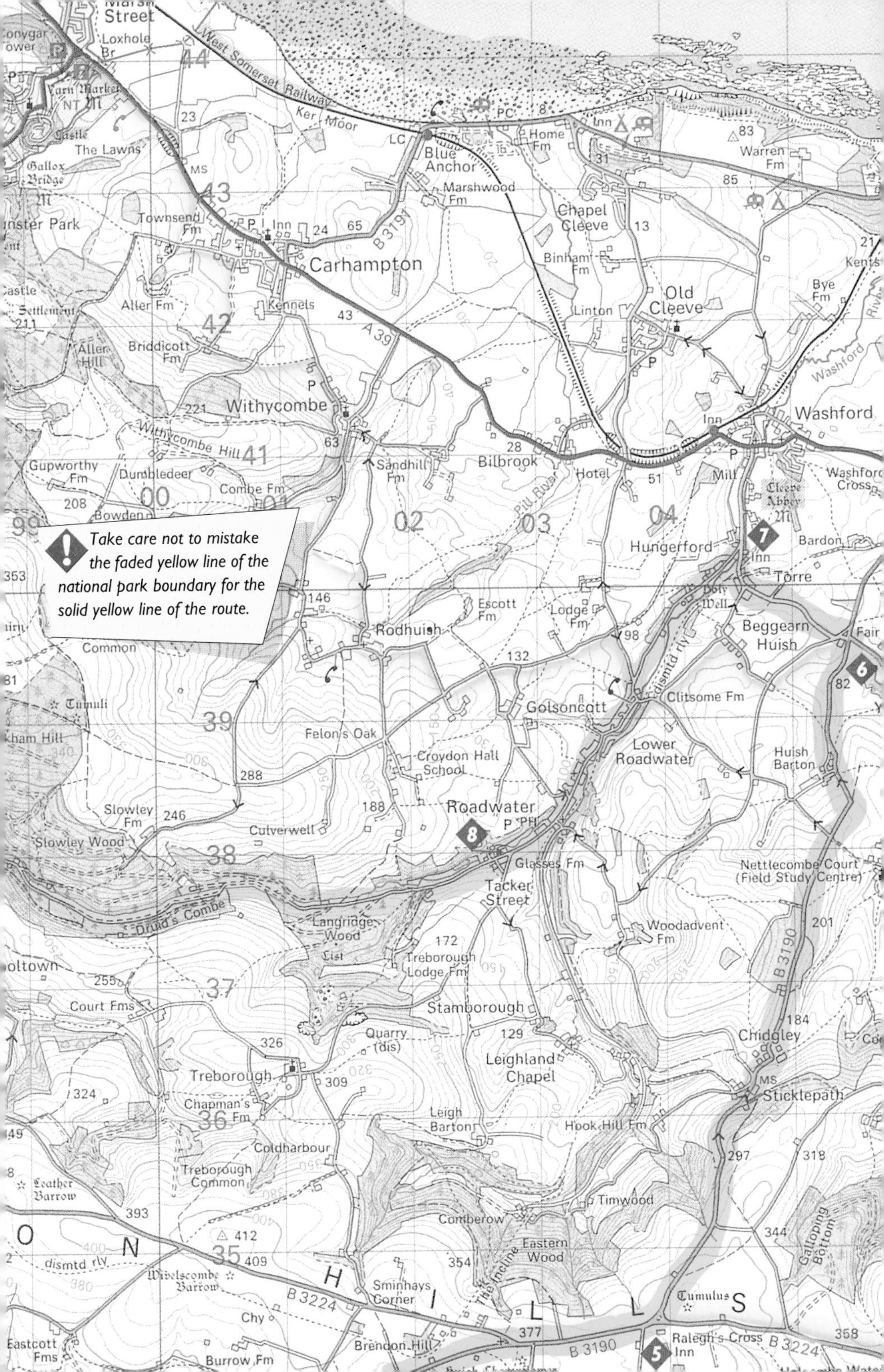
Take care not to mistake the faded yellow line of the national park boundary for the solid yellow line of the route.

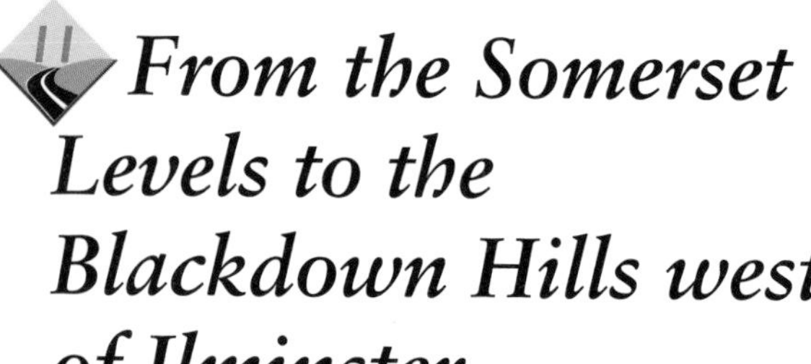

11 From the Somerset Levels to the Blackdown Hills west of Ilminster

The first 10 miles of the ride take you over the Levels of southern Somerset, where all the water drains into the River Isle, hence 'Ilminster', 'Ilton' and 'Isle Abbotts'. The lush pastures of the lowlands give way to the the wooded slopes of the Blackdown Hills. As far as Churchinford, the climbs are long and steady. On the return from Churchinford to Ilminster there are three very sharp ascents but you are more than compensated for your effort by the fabulous views.

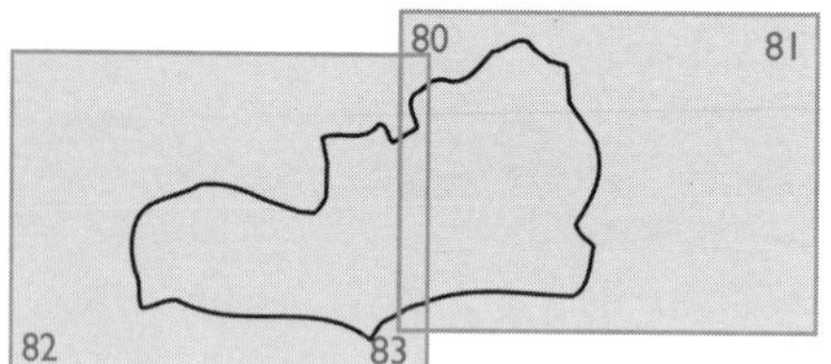

Start

Market Cross in the centre of Ilminster

P Long-term car park south of the centre of town

Distance and grade

32 miles

Moderate/strenuous

Terrain

From the flat Somerset Levels at 50 feet to the Blackdown Hills at 1000 feet, this is a ride of contrasts

Nearest railway

Taunton, 6 miles from the route at Staple Fitzpaine or Crewkerne, 8 miles from Ilminster

Ilminster
Isle Abbotts
Curry Mallet
Hatch Beauchamp
Staple Fitzpaine

Places of interest

Ilminster 1

The spectacular church of St Mary with its Perpendicular tower stands in this market town. It is modelled on Wells Cathedral and inside there is the family tomb of the Wadhams, founders of Wadham College in Oxford.

Refreshments

Plenty of choice in ***Ilminster***
*Greyhound Inn, **Staple Fitzpaine***
*The Bell Inn, **Curry Mallet***
*Hatch Inn, **Hatch Beauchamp***
*York Inn, **Churchstanton***
*Candlelight Inn, **Bishopswood***

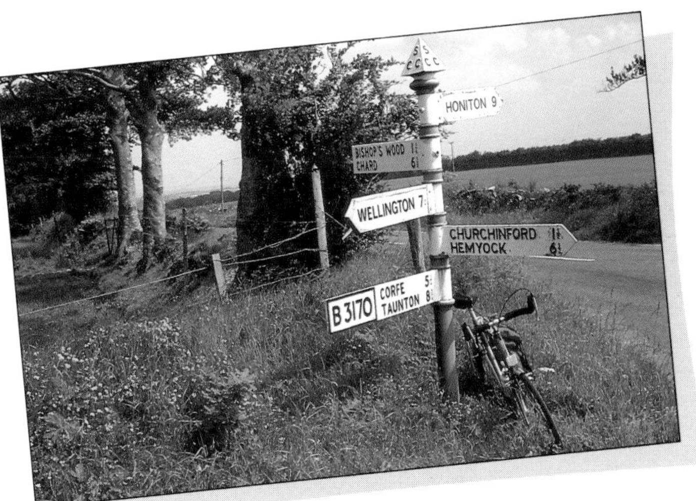

▲ *Near Churchinford*

Holman Clavel

Churchinford

Bishopswood

Sticklepath

Crock Street

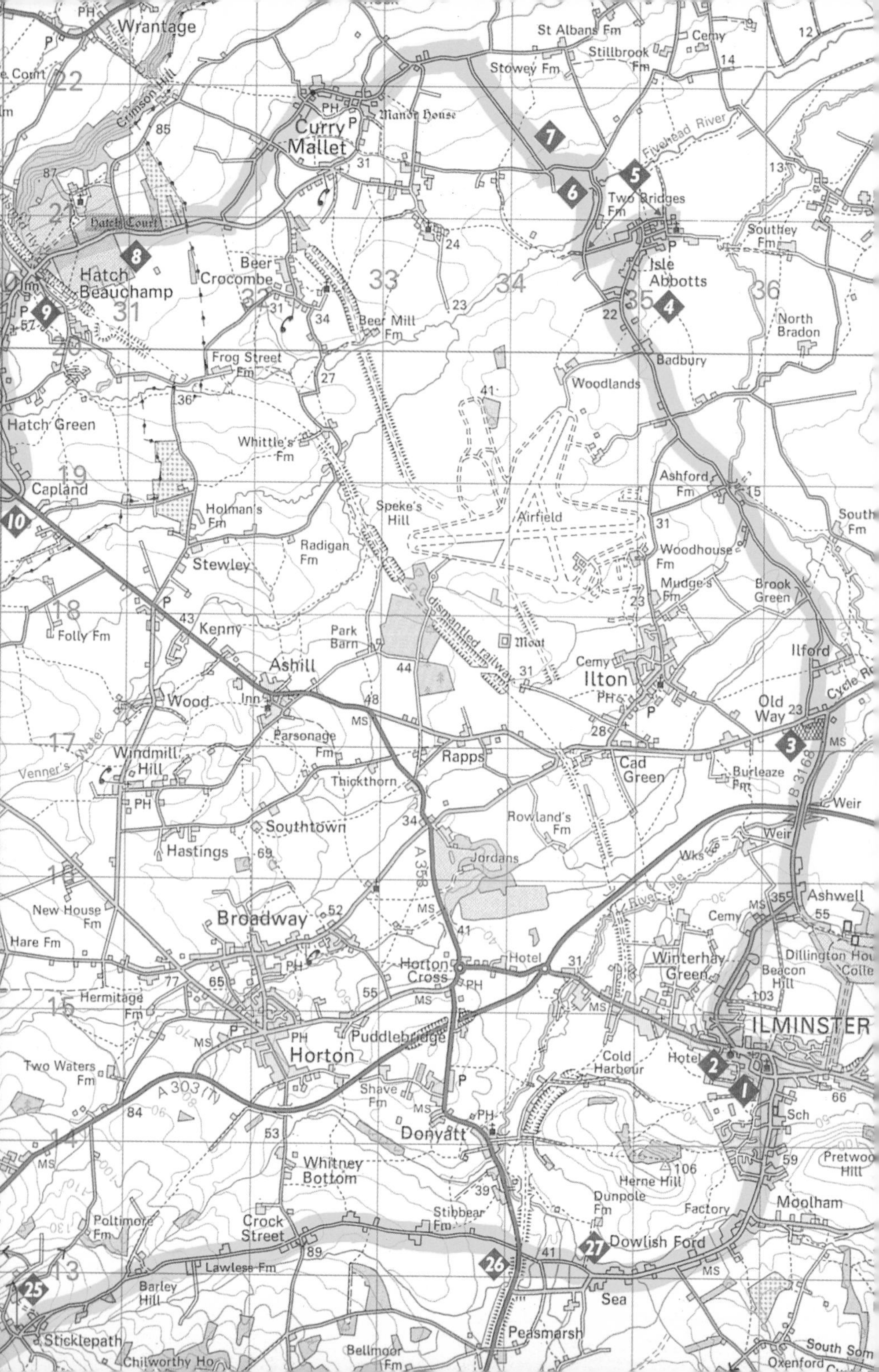

Wrantage
Crimson Hill
Curry Mallet
Manor House
St Albans Fm
Stowey Fm
Stillbrook Fm
Cemy
Fivehead River
Two Bridges Fm
Isle Abbotts
Southey Fm
North Bradon
Badbury
Woodlands
Hatch Court
Hatch Beauchamp
Beer Crocombe
Beer Mill Fm
Frog Street Fm
Hatch Green
Whittle's Fm
Capland
Holman's Fm
Speke's Hill
Airfield
Radigan Fm
Stewley
Ashford Fm
Woodhouse Fm
Mudge's Fm
Brook Green
Folly Fm
Kenny
Park Barn
dismantled railway
Moat
Ashill
Inn
Wood
Ilton
Cemy
Ilford
Old Way
Cycle R
Parsonage Fm
Windmill Hill
Venner's Water
Thickthorn
Rapps
Cad Green
Burleaze Fm
B 3168
Weir
Southtown
Hastings
Rowland's Fm
Jordans
Wks
River Isle
A 358
New House Fm
Hare Fm
Broadway
Horton Cross
Hotel
Winterhay Green
Ashwell
Dillington Hou
Colle
Beacon Hill
Hermitage Fm
Puddlebridge
ILMINSTER
Cold Harbour
Horton
Two Waters Fm
A 303(T)
Shave Fm
Donyatt
Sch
Whitney Bottom
Herne Hill
Pretwo Hill
Moolham
Dunpole Fm
Factory
Poltimore Fm
Crock Street
Stibbear Fm
Dowlish Ford
Lawless Fm
Barley Hill
Sea
Sticklepath
Peasmarsh
Chilworthy Ho
Bellmoor Fm
South Som
Oxenford

1 Follow the one-way system west out of Ilminster 'Langport, Taunton'

2 After 150 yards, at T-j L, then 1st R onto B3168 'Curry Rivel, Langport'

3 ½ mile after crossing bridge over A303, on sharp RH bend, L 'Isle Abbotts, Ilton', then immediately R 'Isle Abbotts'

4 Follow the road right through Isle Abbotts, turning L at the church with its gargoyles

5 Shortly after church, at T-j bear R (in effect SA) then at next T-j R again

6 After ½ mile, at next T-j L 'Curry Mallet, Hatch Beauchamp'

7 After 300 yards 1st R (NS). After ¾ mile, at T-j L (NS) into Curry Mallet

8 At T-j with Halfway House opposite R (NS). Go past Hatch Court into Hatch Beauchamp

9 With the Hatch Inn PH ahead, R then L onto the old A358 'Ilminster, Chard'

10 At the new A358 R then L 'Bickenhall, Staple Fitzpaine'

page 82

25 At offset X-roads R then L (NS)

26 At T-j with A358 look for small path slightly R of SA to gain access to track. Go SA where track joins road

27 At T-j bear L into Ilminster and return to start

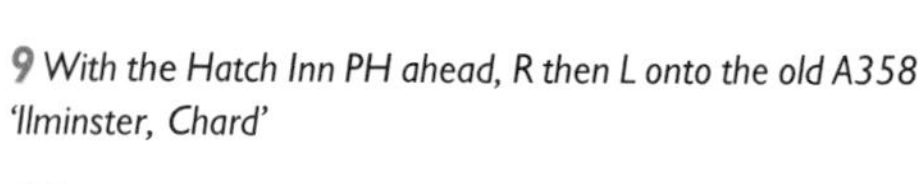

9 With the Hatch Inn PH ahead, R then L onto the old A358 'Ilminster, Chard'

10 At the new A358 R then L 'Bickenhall, Staple Fitzpaine'

11 At T-j L 'Staple Fitzpaine 1½'

12 At X-roads L 'Combe St Nicholas, Chard'

13 Climb 450 feet over 2½ miles. At T-j R 'Wellington, Honiton'

14 Climb further 200 feet to high point of ride at 1000 feet

15 At X-roads with B3170 SA 'Wellington, Churchinford'

16 After ¼ mile 1st L 'Churchinford, Churchstanton'. At X-roads SA 'Bird Garden'

17 At T-j, with masts ahead, L 'Churchinford, Churchstanton'

18 At X-roads by the York Inn in the centre of Churchinford sharply L onto Royston Road 'Bishopswood 3, Ilminster 10'

19 1st of three short, steep climbs (200 feet)

20 At X-roads with B3170 SA 'Bishopswood, Chard'

21 Through Bishopswood. 2nd steep climb (260 feet)

22 At X-roads with A303, **extremely carefully,** *SA 'Crickleaze, Whitestaunton'*

23 3rd steep hill (180 feet) – the worst! At X-roads L (NS)

24 After ½ mile, on sharp LH bend, SA 'Sticklepath ½'. This is a difficult junction: go past it, cross over when you have clear views of the road in both directions, then return to junction

25 At offset X-roads R then L (NS)

page 81

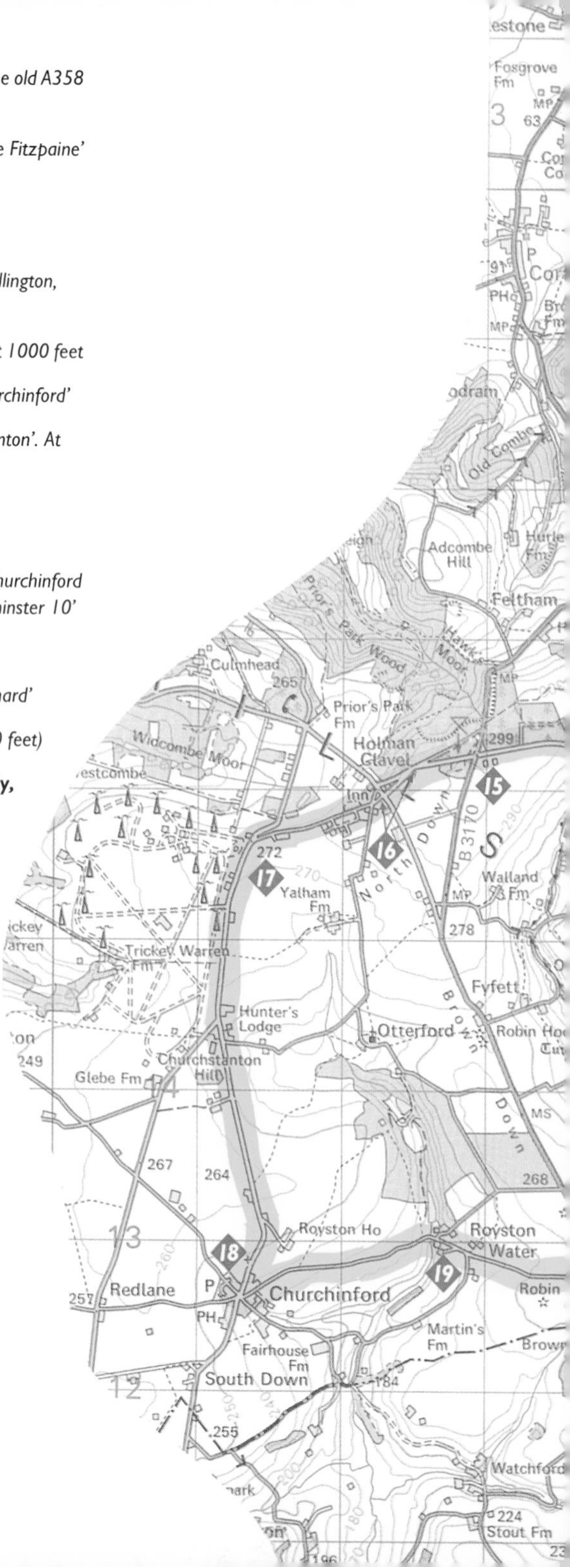

Netherclay
Winter Well
Hill Fm
Stroud's Fm
Slough Green
West Hatch
Boon's Fm
Hatch Park
Heale
Badger Street
Witch Lodge
Frost Street
Animal Centre
Sparks Fm
Streets Farmhouse
Hatch Green
Bickenhall Fm
Park Fm
Pickeridge Hill
Broughton Brook
Forest Lodge
Staple Fm
Batten's Green
Caplanc
Staple Lawns
Lawns Fm
Staple Fitzpaine
Whitty
Bickenhall
Bickenhall Plain
Myrtle Fm
Staple Park Fm
Manor Ho
Abbey Hill
Perry Hall
Staple Park Wood
Lower Hayne
Bow Green
Bulford
Curland
Newtown Fm
Underhill Fm
South Hill Fm
Barrington Hill
Curland Common
Mount Fancy Fm
Ruttersleigh Common
Venner's Fm
Beeches Fm
Staple Common
Forest Trail
Castle Fm
Britty Common
Castle Neroche
Hisbeer's Fm
New Ho
Castle Plain
Old Castle Fm
Hare
Hare Fm
Blackwater
White's Fm
Rydiness Fm
Buckland Fm
Dommett
Dingford Fm
Blindmoor
Beehive Fm
Roses Fm
River Ding
Two Wat
Dommett Moor
Lower Burnt House Fm
Birch Wood
Colley Fm
Buckland Hill
Plyer's Hill
Lane's Fm
Moorseek Fm
Buckland St Mary
The Old Manor
Ham
Rull Fm
Grigg's Fm
Little Hill
Street Ash
Bishopswood
Newtown
Rook's Ho
Fresh Moor
Belcombe
Five Acres
Woodhayne Fm
Combe Beacon Tumulus
Beetham
Coburn's Fm
Longlie Common
Northay Barrow
Combe Head
North Common
Crickleaze Ho
Clifthayne
Cinder Hill
Newbarn Fm
Northay

12 From the hills to the Levels northeast of Ilminster

East from Ilminster the ride passes through some amazing cuttings, near Dinnington, then through the beautiful village of Hinton St George. The one steep climb of the route takes you to the top of Ham Hill, where the views are more than an adequate reward. A steep drop through Stoke Sub Hamdon leads on to Martock and the moors of southern Somerset. The abbey at Muchelney is well worth a visit simply for its incongruous setting in the middle of the Somerset wetlands. The ride passes more lovely houses and deep cuttings on the return via Kingsbury Episcopi and Shepton Beauchamp to Ilminster.

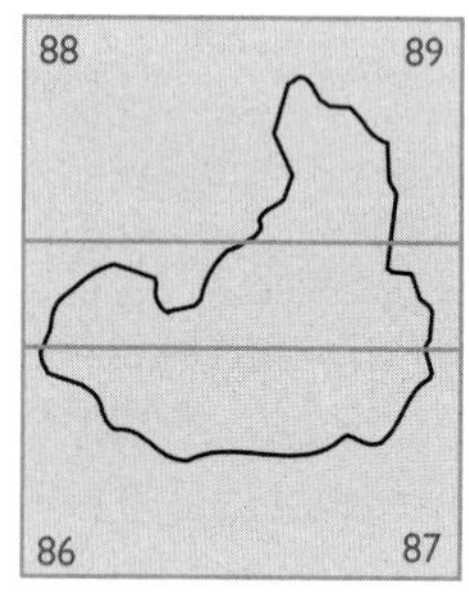

Start

Market Cross in the centre of Ilminster

P Long-term car park south of the centre of town

Distance and grade

29 miles

Moderate

Terrain

Rolling hills near Ilminster, one steep climb up Ham Hill and the flat Somerset Levels north of Martock

Nearest railway

Crewkerne 3½ miles from the route at Merriott

Ilminster · Hinton St George · Merriot · West Chinnock · Stoke Sub Hamdon · Martock

Places of interest

Hamstone Villages

Hinton St George, the Chinnocks, Chiselborough and Stoke Sub Hamdon. The belt of limestone which stretches across south Somerset changes colour and character, from Golden Hamstone in the North to Blue Lias in the South. This stone has been the main building material of past centuries, so the change in the landscape is reflected by the local villages.

▲ *Hinton St George*

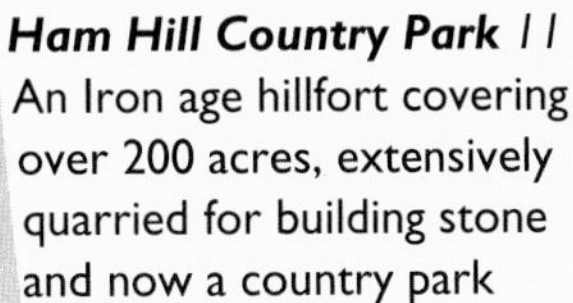

Ham Hill Country Park *11*

An Iron age hillfort covering over 200 acres, extensively quarried for building stone and now a country park offering marvellous views across Somerset. Picnic area and toilets.

Muchelney *15*

Once the site of a great Benedictine abbey founded in AD 950. There is an excavated ground plan of the abbey and church and well preserved remains of a 15th-century cloister and Abbot's lodgings.

Barrington Court Garden

between 17 and 18

Attractive 16th-century 'E' shaped house restored in the early 20th century. In the grounds there is a beautiful walled garden with a kitchen garden supplying produce for the Strode Restaurant that is open for hot and cold lunches and afternoon teas.

Refreshments

Plenty of choice in ***Ilminster***
Poulett Arms PH, ***Hinton St George***
Cat Head Inn, ***Chiselborough***
Prince of Wales PH, ***Ham Hill***
Half Moon PH, Fleur de Lys PH,
Stoke Sub Hamdon
Plenty of choice in ***Martock***
Wyndham Arms PH,
Kingsbury Episcopi
Royal Oak PH, ***Barrington***

Muchelney

West Lambrook

Shepton Beauchamp

Barrington

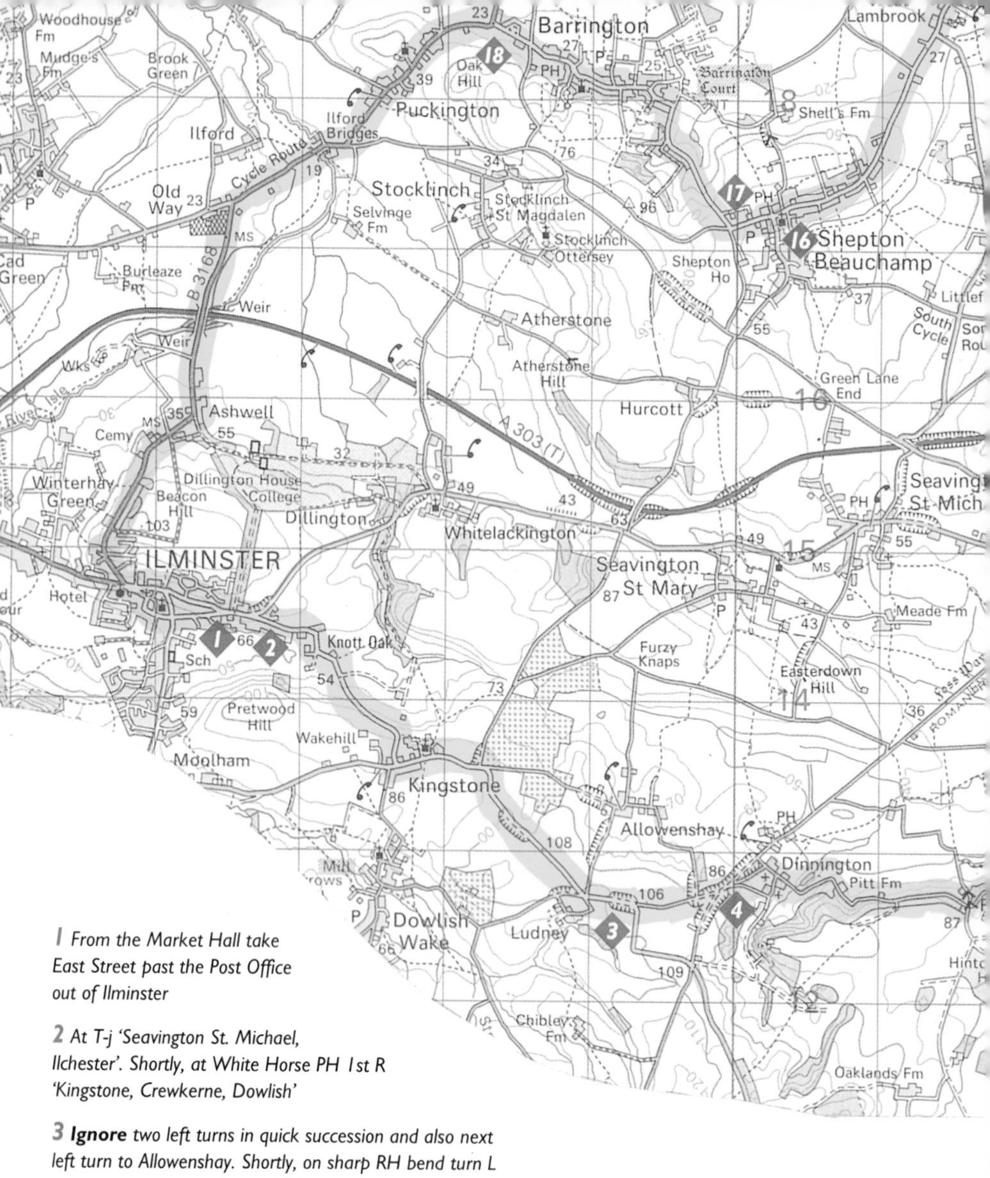

1 From the Market Hall take East Street past the Post Office out of Ilminster

2 At T-j 'Seavington St. Michael, Ilchester'. Shortly, at White Horse PH 1st R 'Kingstone, Crewkerne, Dowlish'

3 ***Ignore*** *two left turns in quick succession and also next left turn to Allowenshay. Shortly, on sharp RH bend turn L 'Dinnington. Unsuitable for HGVs'*

4 At T-j bear L (NS) then shortly 2nd R 'Hinton St George 1½, Merriott 2¾'. Wonderful sunken lanes. At next T-j with letter box in wall opposite R (NS)

5 1 mile after Hinton St George, at T-j R 'Crewkerne' then 1st L onto Church Street 'Scotts Nurseries'

6 At T-j in Merriott L 'Martock, Ilchester'

7 At T-j with A356 R then 1st L 'West Chinnock, Middle Chinnock'

8 At T-j at the end of Scotts Way L onto Lower Street

9 Through West Chinnock. Ignore 1st turn right by triangle of grass to Middle Chinnock and follow signs for Chiselborough. Shortly after brow of hill and LH bend at the start of Chiselborough turn R opposite bus shelter 'Norton, Ham Hill'

10 On sharp LH bend R (in effect SA) 'Little Norton, Ham Hill, Unsuitable for HGVs'. Steep climb, brilliant views

11 *At T-j at top of hill L (NS). Picnic or stop for refreshment at Prince of Wales PH*

12 *Descend into Stoke Sub Hamdon. At T-j L then 1st R onto North Street 'Martock'*

 **page 88**

16 *Follow this road for 6½ miles through Kingsbury into Shepton Beauchamp. At Duke of York PH bear R (in effect SA) on Great Lane up an amazing road cut into the 'bowels of Somerset'*

17 *At X-roads R 'Barrington, Langport, Taunton'*

18 *At T-j with B3168 bear L 'Puckington, Ilminster' to return to Ilminster*

11 *At T-j at top of hill L (NS). Picnic or stop for refreshment at Prince of Wales PH*

12 *Descend into Stoke Sub Hamdon. At T-j L then 1st R onto North Street 'Martock'*

13 *After 1½ miles, at T-j with B3165, opposite Brooks Garage, R 'Martock'*

14 ***Easy to miss.*** *Through Martock. 1½ miles after the end of the village L 'Muchelney, Muchelney Abbey'*

15 *At T-j L 'Muchelney Pottery' (or R to visit Muchelney Abbey)*

16 *Follow this road for 6½ miles through Kingsbury into Shepton Beauchamp. At Duke of York PH bear R (in effect SA) on Great Lane up an amazing road cut into the 'bowels of Somerset'*

17 *At X-roads R 'Barrington, Langport, Taunton'*

18 *At T-j with B3168 bear L 'Puckington, Ilminster' to return to Ilminster*

page 87

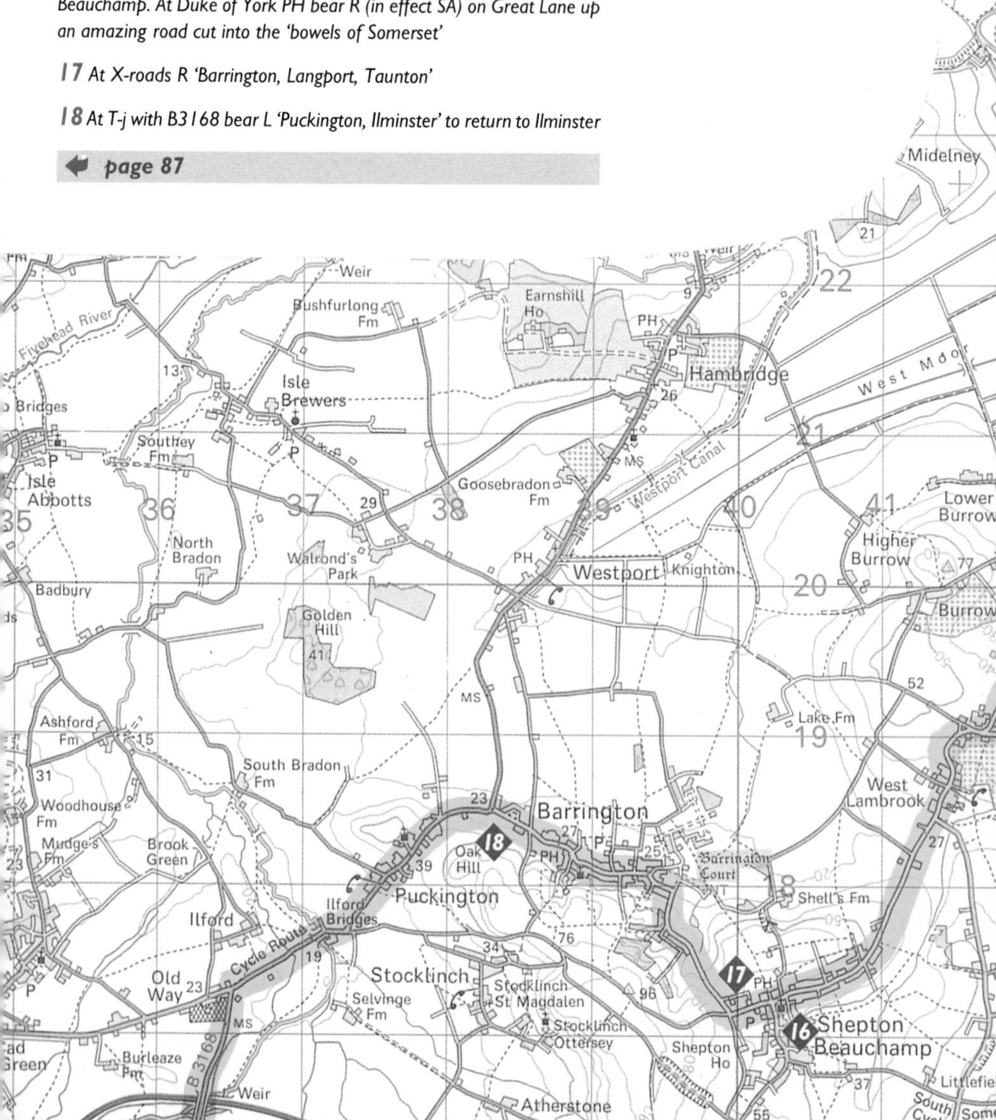

Huish Episcopi
A 372
Pibsbury
Horsey Fm
Bicknell's Br
Muchelney Level
Cycle Route
Manor House Fm
Long Sutton
Knole
Plot Dairy Fm
Hay Moor
Priest's Ho
Abbey
Muchelney
15
Lame Hill
Wet Moor
Little Load
King's Moor
Load Bridge
River Yeo (Ivel)
Thorney Moor
Muchelney Ham
Long Load
Witcombe Bottom
Thorney
Sluice
Stapleton Mead Fm
dismtd rly
14
B3165
Milton
Witcombe
SOUTH SOMERSET DISTRIC
Kingsbury Episcopi
Stapleton
Highway
River Parrett
Ash
Stembridge
Coat
Cycle Route
Gawbridge Mill
Martock
Foldhill Fms
Halfway House
Southay
Hills Fm
East Lambrook
Weir
13
Garden
Works Sluice
Hurst
Foss Way
Roman Road
Wellham's Mill
Mid Lambrook
Lambrook Brook
Bower Hinton
Stoke Sub Hamdon
West Stoke
East Stoke
Stoodham
Ringwell Hill
Joylers Fm
Cripple Hill
Priory
Compton Durville
Hospl
12
Leland Trail
Hedgecock Hill
A 303 (T)
Ham Hill Country Park
South Petherton
Petherton Br
A 356
11
Sluice
Fort
Cycle Route
Cemy
Norton Sub

13 Valleys and downland west of Wilton

Three river valleys (the Wylye, the Nadder and the Ebble) run almost parallel to the west of Wilton. This ride heads out along the valley formed by the River Wylye, passing several beautiful thatched houses in the villages of Great Wishford and Hanging Langford before turning south and crossing two downland ridges with fine views to reach the Ebble Valley at Fifield Bavant. The route now goes east to Bishopstone and recrosses the final ridge to return to Wilton.

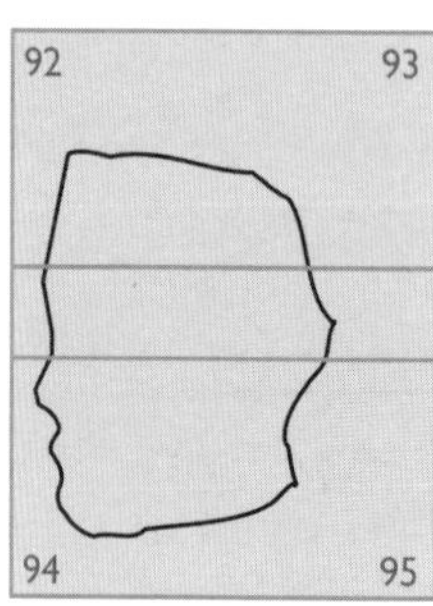

This ride can easily be linked with the ride east of Wilton, which circles Salisbury, to form a 64-mile loop. The link point is at instruction 10.

Start

The Square, Wilton

P On side streets or on roads out of town

Distance and grade

25 miles

Easy/moderate

Terrain

Two stretches of very gentle valley cycling linked by four climbs, the first, of 400 feet, south from Wylye; the second, of 200 feet, between Dinton and Fovant; the third (the steepest), of 300 feet, south of Fovant; and the final one, of 330 feet, north from Bishopstone

Nearest railway

Salisbury, 3 miles from Wilton

Wilton
Great Wishford
Hanging Langford
Wylye
Di

Places of interest

***Wilton** 1*

The word Wiltshire is derived from Wilton-shire. Wilton was King Egbert's capital and the foundations of the Royal Palace are thought to lie beneath the Georgian Houses in Kingsbury Square. For many centuries Wilton has been best known for its carpet-making and the Royal Wilton Carpet Factory is famous throughout the world.

Refreshments

*Queens Head PH ♥, **Broad Chalke***
*Penruddock Arms PH, **Dinton***
*The Bell PH ♥♥, **Wylye***
*Royal Oak PH ♥, **Great Wishford***
*Wiltons PH ♥, plenty of choice in **Wilton***

***Wilton House** 1*

Close to the start of the route, Wilton House stands on the site of a Saxon abbey which was given to William Herbert (later the 1st Earl of Pembroke) by Henry VIII. The original Tudor house and its contents were almost completely destroyed in a fire in about 1647. Rebuilding started immediately under the supervision of Inigo Jones and was completed in about 1653. The house is famous for its 'double cube' room and Palladian bridge. Its treasures include family portraits painted for the 4th Earl by Van Dyck, as well as paintings by Reynolds, Rembrandt, Rubens and Poussin and furniture by Chippendale and William Kent.

***Philipps House, Dinton** 5*

A National Trust property lying to the west of the route designed by Jeffrey Wyattville and completed in 1816.

Fovant
Broad Chalke
Stoke Farthing

Stony Hill
Parry's Field Barn
Deptford Field Barn
Deptford Down
Yarnbury Castle fort
A 303 (T)
Fisherton de la Mere
Bapton
Wylye
Deptford
Tumulus
Little Down
Bathampton Ho
Ballington Manor
Steeple Langford Cow Down
Clifford Bottom
Wylye Valley
R Wylye
Weir
East Clyffe
Steeple Langford
A 36 (T)
Hanging Langford
Little Langford
Bilbury Fm
Bilbury Rings
Wylye Down
Church end Ring
Penning Bottom
East Castle
Tumulus
West Hill
Hanging Langford Camp
Upper Farm Down
Grovely Castle
Field System
Ebsbury
Ebsbury Copse
ROMAN ROAD
Middle Hills
Oakley Fm
Grovely Wood
Grovely Lodge
Grovely Fm
Teffont Field Buildings
Hamshill Ditch
Marshwood Fm
Crouch's Down
SALISBURY D
Wick Ball Camp
Philipps House
Dinton
Manor Fm
Baverstock
Manor
Inn
B 3089
Teffont Manor
Sluice
Barford St Martin
Hurdcott Ho
R Nadder
Mill Fm
Cemy

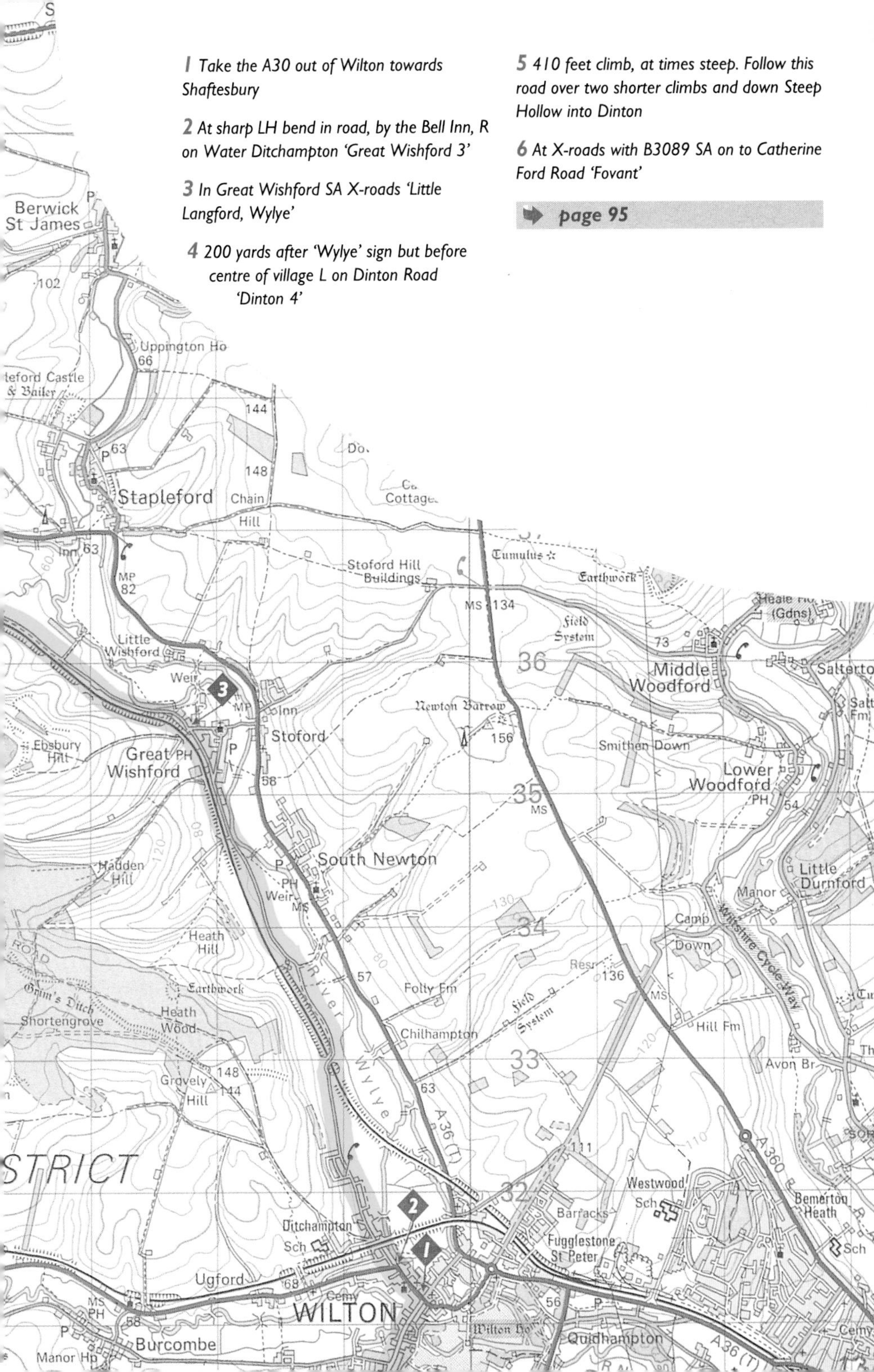

1 Take the A30 out of Wilton towards Shaftesbury

2 At sharp LH bend in road, by the Bell Inn, R on Water Ditchampton 'Great Wishford 3'

3 In Great Wishford SA X-roads 'Little Langford, Wylye'

4 200 yards after 'Wylye' sign but before centre of village L on Dinton Road 'Dinton 4'

5 410 feet climb, at times steep. Follow this road over two shorter climbs and down Steep Hollow into Dinton

6 At X-roads with B3089 SA on to Catherine Ford Road 'Fovant'

page 95

Teffont Field Buildings
Marshwood Fm
Dinton
Baverstock
Manor Fm
Crouch's Down
SALISBURY
Philipps House
Wick Ball Camp
Teffont Manor
Barford St Martin
Hurdcott Ho
River Nadder
Mill Fm
Compton Wood
Fovant Wood
Compton Park
Compton Chamberlayne
Naishes Fm
Upper Hurdcott Fm
Fir Hill
Fovant
Greystones
Manor Fm
Burcombe Ivers
East Fm
Regimental Badges
Chiselbury
West Fm
Compton Down
Fovant Down
Hydon Hill
Hut Bottom
Little Down
Flamstone Fm
Knapp Down
Tumuli
Field Barn
Stoke Down
Fovant Hut
Gurston Down
Fifield Down
North Barn
Tumulus
Broad Chalke
Stoke Fm
Stoke Farthing
Knighton Manor
Gurston Fm
Knapp Fm
Fifield Bavant
Mount Sorrel
Wiltshire Cycle Way
Church Bottom
Knighton Hill
Knighton Hill Fm
Ebbesborne Wake
Mead End
Hill Fm
Middleton Hill
Rookhay Fm
Bowerchalke
Knowle Hill
Drove

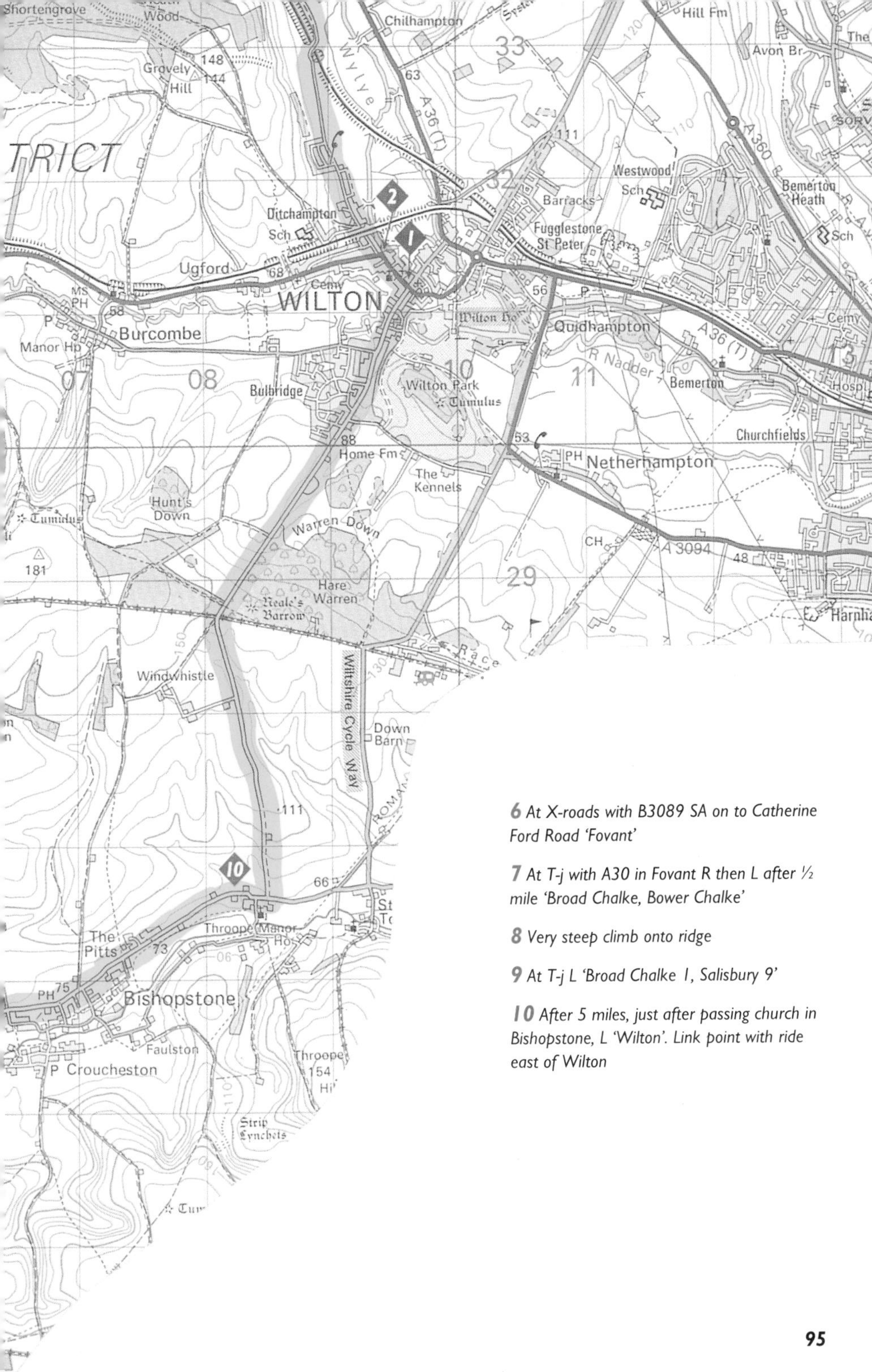

6 At X-roads with B3089 SA on to Catherine Ford Road 'Fovant'

7 At T-j with A30 in Fovant R then L after ½ mile 'Broad Chalke, Bower Chalke'

8 Very steep climb onto ridge

9 At T-j L 'Broad Chalke 1, Salisbury 9'

10 After 5 miles, just after passing church in Bishopstone, L 'Wilton'. Link point with ride east of Wilton

14 A circle around Salisbury via Alderbury, Porton and the Woodfords

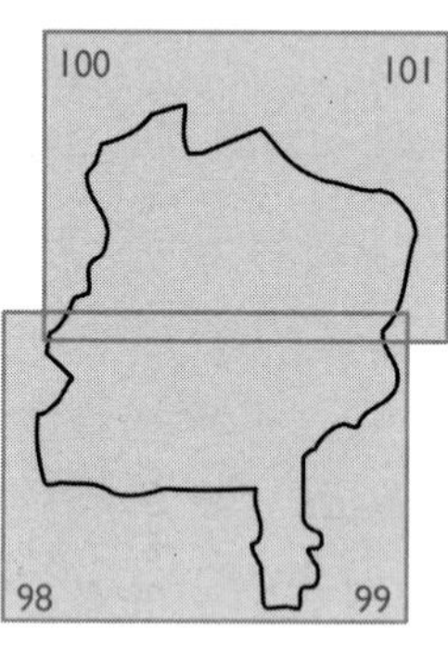

Starting from the historic town of Wilton, the ride leaves the Nadder Valley and crosses the downland to the south to drop into the lovely Ebble Valley. It goes east through Odstock and Nunton and follows the valley of the River Avon to the first available bridge crossing at Downton, then back north to Alderbury. The route enters a military landscape, passing the research units at Porton Down and Boscombe Down, which may well send a shiver up your spine. On the other side of the A345 the route continues along the River Avon through the charming Woodford villages before a last downland climb to return to Wilton.

Start

The Square, Wilton

P On side streets or on roads out of town

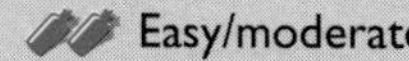

Distance and grade

39 miles

Easy/moderate

Terrain

Three climbs of 250 feet: one south from Wilton to cross the ridge, the second from Alderbury northeast towards Pitton and the third, the least lovable, coming at the end of the ride, between Lower Woodford and the A360

Nearest railway

Salisbury, 2 miles

Refreshments

Silver Plough PH, **Pitton**
Fox and Goose PH, **Coombe Bissett**
Yew Tree PH, **Odstock**

Wilton
Coombe Bissett
Nunton
Alderbury

Places of interest

Salisbury 1

Salisbury, the county town of Wiltshire, lies at the heart of this route. It is situated at the confluence of the rivers Avon, Bourne, Nadder and Wylye and remains a thriving market town with many places of interest.

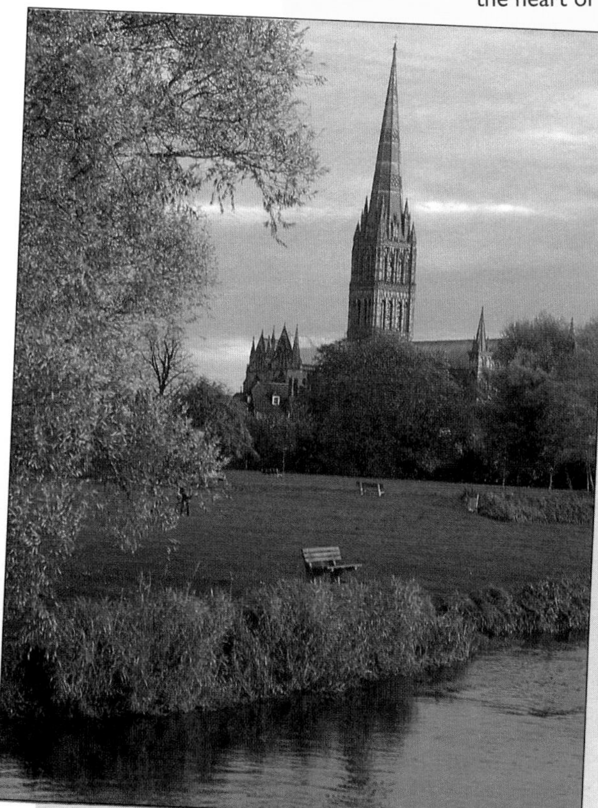

▲ *Salisbury Cathedral*

Salisbury Cathedral 1

The cathedral was refounded in Salisbury in 1220 and took 38 years to complete and the spire that towers to 404 feet was added by the end of the century. It has a uniformity of style and there is an entrance for every month of the year, a window for every day and a column for every hour. Among the tombs within the cathedral is that of William Longespere who witnessed the signing of the Magna Carta of which one of the four remaining copies is kept in the library over the east walk.

Old Sarum

This lies to the north of the present city and was the site of the original cathedral and a castle. Friction between the Church and State in such close proximity led to the refoundation of the cathedral in its present location and the subsequent decline of Old Sarum.

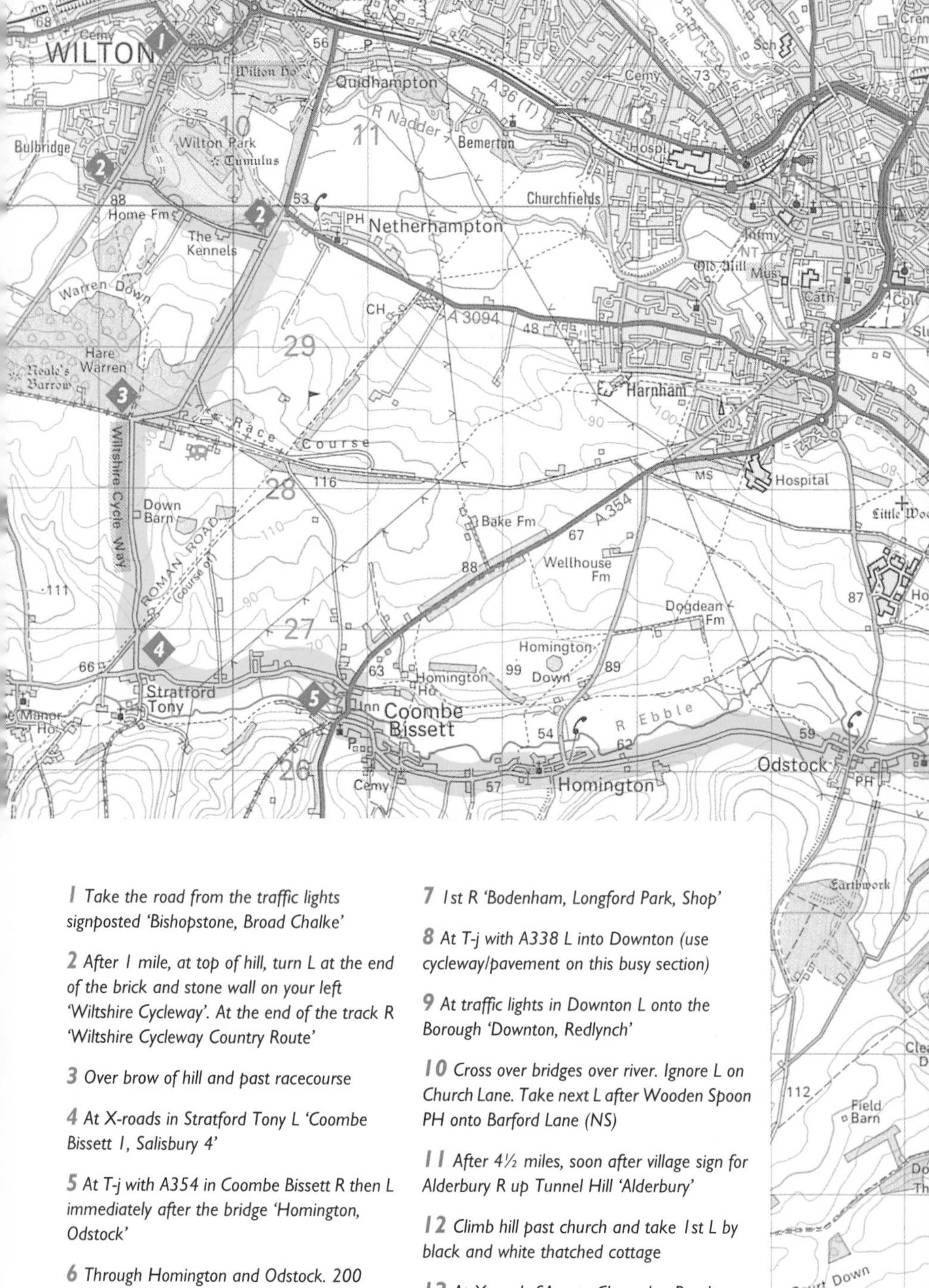

1 Take the road from the traffic lights signposted 'Bishopstone, Broad Chalke'

2 After 1 mile, at top of hill, turn L at the end of the brick and stone wall on your left 'Wiltshire Cycleway'. At the end of the track R 'Wiltshire Cycleway Country Route'

3 Over brow of hill and past racecourse

4 At X-roads in Stratford Tony L 'Coombe Bissett 1, Salisbury 4'

5 At T-j with A354 in Coombe Bissett R then L immediately after the bridge 'Homington, Odstock'

6 Through Homington and Odstock. 200 yards after Radnor Arms in Nunton, on sharp LH bend R (NS) by thatched wall. At X-roads with A338 'New Hall Hospital'

7 1st R 'Bodenham, Longford Park, Shop'

8 At T-j with A338 L into Downton (use cycleway/pavement on this busy section)

9 At traffic lights in Downton L onto the Borough 'Downton, Redlynch'

10 Cross over bridges over river. Ignore L on Church Lane. Take next L after Wooden Spoon PH onto Barford Lane (NS)

11 After 4½ miles, soon after village sign for Alderbury R up Tunnel Hill 'Alderbury'

12 Climb hill past church and take 1st L by black and white thatched cottage

13 At X-roads SA onto Clarendon Road, 'Farley, Pitton'. Cross bridge over dual carriageway. After 1 mile 1st left 'Farley, Pitton'

14 *At X-roads in Farley L onto Parsonage Hill 'Pitton'*

15 *In Pitton 200 yards past Silver Plough PH R onto High Street 'Winterslow'*

page 100

15 In Pitton 200 yards past Silver Plough PH R onto High Street 'Winterslow'

16 At X-roads SA 'Andover, Stockbridge'

17 At X-roads with A30 SA through gates to cross Porton Down

18 Through Porton to X-roads with A338. SA 'Amesbury 5'

19 50 yards before the busy A345 turn R onto track alongside perimeter fence by Crash Exit sign 'Byway to Amesbury'. The first 400 yards are the toughest. At T-j with road L. At X-roads with A345 SA

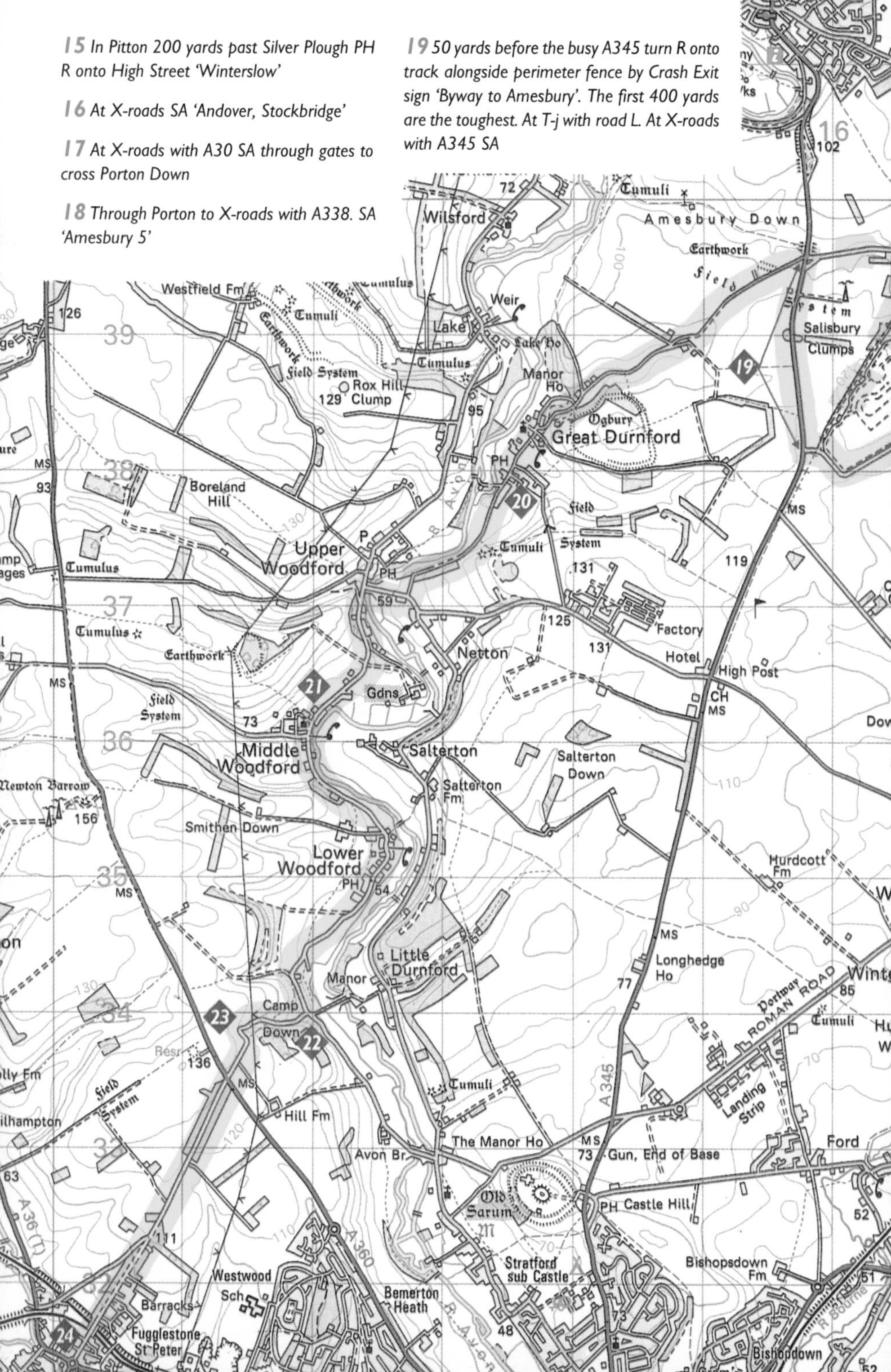

20 *Through Great Durnford, at T-j R 'Woodford, Wilton', then L at T-j by Bridge at Woodford PH 'Salisbury, Wilton'*

21 *For link to route west of Wilton, at telephone box in Middle Woodford R 'Great Wishford 3'*

22 *For return to Wilton, go through Middle Woodford and 1 mile after Lower Woodford R 'Wilton'*

23 *Steep climb to X-roads. SA 'Wilton 2'*

24 *At roundabout SA 'Town Centre'*

Steep Cotswold hills between Bristol and Bath

A short but demanding ride, this route gives you hard climbs and fast descents, panoramic views and a great dollop of mud near Lower Hamswell. The southern end of the Cotswolds near Bath has some of the steepest roads in the region and the off-road tracks are similar, with hillsides falling away very steeply either side of Lansdown Hill. The climbs are rewarded with fine views into the Avon Valley.

Start

Upton Cheyney, just north of the A431 Bristol to Bath Road

P Near the Upton Inn in Upton Cheyney.

Distance and grade

11 miles

Moderate/strenuous

Terrain

Lots of steep climbs and descents. Mud near Lower Hamswell

Nearest railway

Bath or Keynsham

Refreshments

Upton PH, ***Upton Cheyney***

Upton Cheyney

Brockham End

Off-road riding tips

- Padded shorts and gloves make off-road riding more comfortable
- If there is any possibility of rain, take something waterproof. Never underestimate the effects of wind-chill when you are wet, even in summer
- In wet and cold conditions keep a layer of warm clothes next to the skin – thermal underwear or wool
- After fixing a puncture, check the inside of the tyre for embedded thorns before replacing the inner tube. A screwdriver is useful for winkling out difficult thorns
- Lower your saddle when going down steep off-road sections, keep the pedals level, stand up out of the saddle to let your legs absorb the bumps and keep your weight over the rear wheel
- Carry a water bottle in the bottle carrier and keep it filled, particularly on hot days
- Take a compass with you for crossing moorland or in poor visibility and know how to use it
- Good equipment doesn't make you a good cyclist. The only bad cyclists are those who show no consideration to others, whether by weaving around, failing to indicate or riding on pavements in on-road situations, or by failing to follow the countryside code, and showing no respect to walkers and horseriders when off-road

...gridge Tadwick Lower Hamswell

1 *Go uphill from the Upton Inn for 400 yards*

2 *As the road swings left, bear R (in effect SA) up Lansdown Lane*

3 *Climb steadily on tarmac then track to the golf course*

4 *Keep wall and wood to your left and golf course to your right. Cross a major track at right angles (this is the drive to the golf club, a private road) and continue until reaching a junction of tracks at the end of the wood. Turn sharply L alongside the edge of the wood (maybe muddy)*

5 *At T-j with tarmac R. At T-j with the road R for 150 yards*

6 *Just before reaching the second clump of trees, L through a wicket gate and across the field towards the gate in the stone wall*

7 *Before the signpost, bear R down the broad track. This soon becomes a fine descent*

8 *At T-j by barn at the bottom R. At T-j with road L. At next T-j L again*

9 *Climb for ¾ mile, ignore the 1st lane/No Through Road on the left to Tadwick Farm. Continue climbing steeply for 300 yards and take the next L*

10 *After 200 yards, as the lane turns left more steeply downhill towards the farm, by a metal gate, turn R uphill on to track which follows hedgerow on the left. After 100 yards, bear L downhill. Maybe rutted and/or muddy*

11 *Cross the stream and climb on tarmac. At X-roads SA*

12 *At next X-roads SA 'Beach 1, Upton Cheyney 1½'*

13 *1st R 'Beach 1', then after 100 yards, bear R on the No Through Road. Tarmac becomes track. At the bottom, follow the stone stream bed to the L. You will probably have to push for a short stretch*

14 *Descend to cross the stream and follow the track as it climbs, levels out then turns to tarmac at Coldharbour Farm. At T-j with road L then immediately L 'Upton Cheyney'*

15 *At X-roads SA 'Upton Cheyney' to return to start*

Ancient earthworks around Avebury

This ride would be easy but for the wild Wansdyke section which is well worth doing for the sense of history and magnificent views although it may involve some pushing. It links the superb ridges of Cherhill Down and Wansdyke and even takes in a section of the most famous ancient road of all in this area: the first couple of miles of the Ridgeway.

Start

Red Lion PH, Avebury

P Follow signs from centre of Avebury

Distance and grade

19 miles

Moderate

▲ *Avebury village and stone circle*

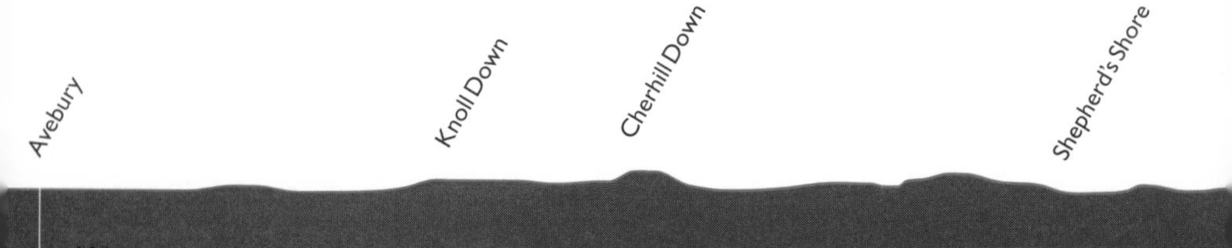

Avebury

Knoll Down

Cherhill Down

Shepherd's Shore

Terrain

Chalk downland, ancient tracks, rough section on Wansdyke. Climb of 300 feet on to Cherhill Down, otherwise mainly ridge riding.

Nearest railway

Pewsey, 5 miles from the Wansdyke section lying to the south of East Kennett

Places of interest

Avebury 1

The main part of the village lies within a Neolithic stone circle encompassing an area of about 28 acres. The outer stone circle once comprised up to 100 stones, some weighing as much as 100 tons. The site does not share the fame of its neighbour Stonehenge, but its importance was regarded by the antiquarian John Aubrey (1629-97) as great enough for him to persuade Charles II to visit, stating that it 'exceeded Stonehenge as a Cathedral exceeds a parish church'. The Alexander Keiller museum in the village tells much of the story of Avebury and other monuments nearby.

Silbury Hill

South of Avebury is Silbury Hill, the largest man-made mound in Europe.

West Kennet Long Barrow

This 5000-year-old site is one of the largest chambered tombs in Britain.

Refreshments

Red Lion PH, tea shops, ***Avebury***

East Kennett

1 With your back to the PH, R down the no through road towards the church

2 100 yards after the church on the right and just past the Old Vicarage to your left turn R onto tarmac lane. Road narrows to path. At fork by white railings bear R. At triangle of grass by Swan Cottage bear R (in effect SA)

3 Opposite barns on left turn R 'Ancient Monument'

4 Ignore gate on right to Windmill Hill. Go SA in same direction onto grassy track. Shortly after brow of hill enter copse and turn immediately L sharply back on yourself. At T-j with better stone-based track bear L (in effect SA)

5 At X-roads with main road (A4) SA onto track. After 400 yards 1st track R along top of ridge (earthworks)

6 At T-j at end L uphill to barn and through gate on right. At top of hill follow main track round to the R for the monument and fine views **or** *carry SA onto grassy track for continuation of route*

7 Follow in same direction with earthworks on the right. Descend through two bridlegates towards strip of pine trees

8 At start of pine trees turn R towards masts. Follow fence for 1½ miles. Ignore two bridlegates to the left with tracks climbing steeply to the masts. Continue into and out of woodland on contouring track

9 At sign for Morgan's Hill Nature Reserve sharply L back on yourself through bridlegate

10 Follow Wansdyke, the obvious earthworks, towards the main road (A361). At a copse you will have to detour L then R to return to route. (This section may be very rough)

11 Cross road then L and R towards new house to get up onto Wan dyke. The going is very rough to begin with and you will have to push but does improve

12 For the next 6 miles the route follows Wansdyke. The earthworks themselves are impossible to lose; the best route,however, may be to the R, to the L or on top of the ridge and comprehensive instructions would be meaningless. It is a beautiful section, so it does not matter if it is slow

13 The route descends to the Alton Barnes-Marlborough road, bearing away to the R of Wansdyke for the last few hundred yards

14 At T-j with road L then after ¾ mile 1st road L 'West Overton 2, East Kennett 1'

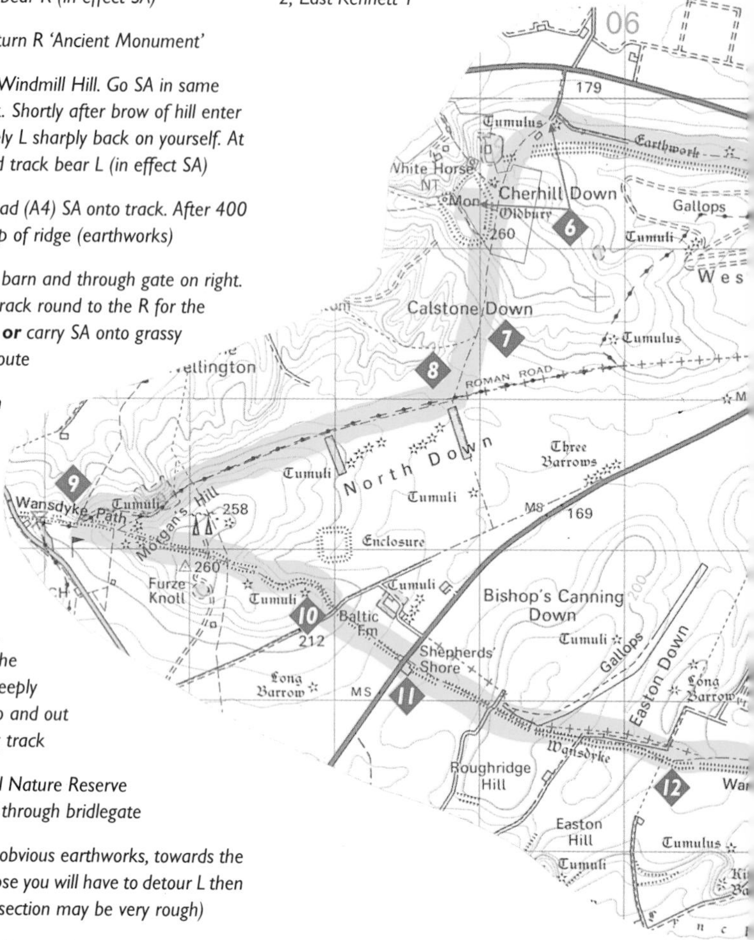

15 In East Kennett, just before 'School' sign R 'West Overton 1' then very shortly L alongside stone wall

16 At X-roads with main road (A4) SA on to Ridgeway. Ignore 1st byway to the left as you climb hill. After 1½ miles next L on broad track 'Byway' to return to Red Lion PH in Avebury

17 Cross main road (A4) on to Ridgeway and take 2nd L (byway) down into Avebury

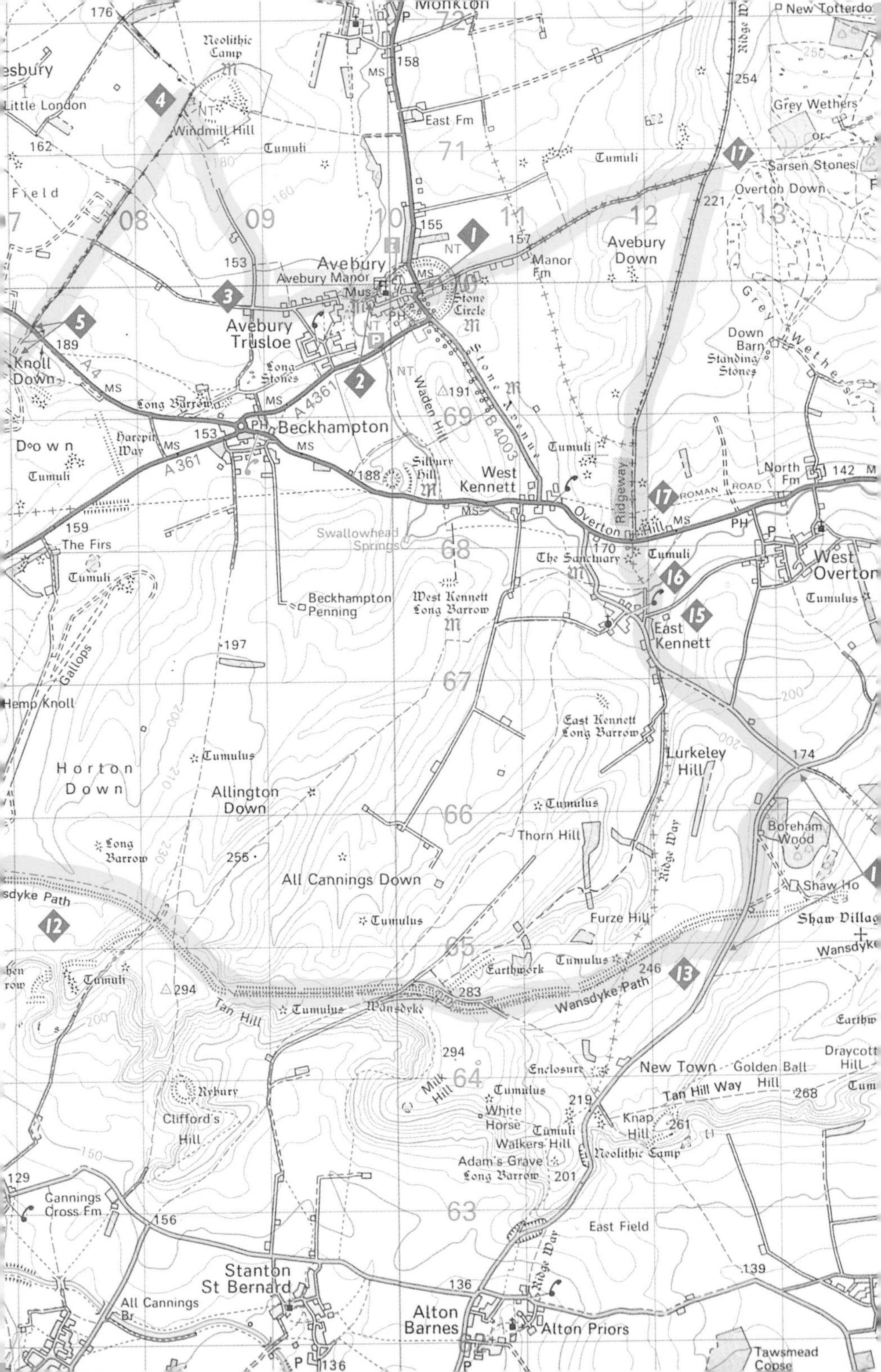
Monkton
New Totterdown
Neolithic Camp
Windmill Hill
Little London
Tumuli
East Fm
Grey Wethers
Sarsen Stones
Overton Down
Avebury
Avebury Manor
Mus
Stone Circle
Manor Fm
Avebury Down
Avebury Trusloe
Long Stones
Knoll Down
Long Barrow
Beckhampton
Waden Hill
Stone Avenue
Down Barn
Standing Stones
Harepit Way
Down
Tumuli
Silbury Hill
West Kennett
Ridgeway
North Fm
Roman Road
Overton Hill
Swallowhead Springs
The Sanctuary
The Firs
West Overton
Tumulus
Beckhampton Penning
West Kennett Long Barrow
East Kennett
Gallops
Hemp Knoll
East Kennett Long Barrow
Lurkeley Hill
Horton Down
Allington Down
Boreham Wood
Thorn Hill
Long Barrow
Ridge Way
All Cannings Down
Wansdyke Path
Shaw Ho
Furze Hill
Shaw Village
Wansdyke
Earthwork
Tan Hill
Wansdyke Path
Milk Hill
Enclosure
New Town
Golden Ball Hill
Draycott Hill
Rybury
Tan Hill Way
Clifford's Hill
White Horse
Knap Hill
Walkers Hill
Neolithic Camp
Adam's Grave Long Barrow
Cannings Cross Fm
East Field
Stanton St Bernard
All Cannings Br
Alton Barnes
Alton Priors
Tawsmead Copse
A4
A4361
A361
B4003

Over Dundry Hill and along little-known tracks southwest of Bristol

This ride covers a wide variety of terrain very close to Bristol and climbs to the top of the ridge that forms Dundry Hill. There are two steep climbs and one muddy descent. The route provides good views across the Bristol Channel to Wales and back over Bristol.

Start

The Angel PH, Long Ashton, southwest of Bristol

P Along the Long Ashton road or in Ashton Court

Distance and grade

17 miles

Moderate

Terrain

Two steep climbs – 450 feet to the top of Barrow Hill, 500 feet to the top of Dundry Hill. **Warning**: *much of this ride, particularly the first off-road section on Barrow Hill and the descent from Dundry can be very muddy through the winter and after prolonged rain*

Nearest railway

Bristol Temple Meads

Refreshments

The Angel PH, **Long Ashton**
The Bungalow Inn PH, **Redhill** *(just off the route, south of instruction 8)*
Crown Inn PH, **Regil** *(just off the route, south of instruction 12)*
Princes Motto PH, **Barrow Gurney**

Long Ashton

Barrow Hill

Lulsgate Bottom

Kingdown

Off-road riding tips

- Keep some spare dry clothes and shoes in the car to change into and carry some bin liners in the car to put dirty, wet clothes in
- In very wet weather keep other possessions dry by carrying them in two sets of plastic bags
- If your brake blocks look as though they are wearing thin, take a spare set with you. New brake blocks are much cheaper than new rims
- Experiment with saddle height, forwards and backwards adjustment of saddle, tilt of saddle up or down and height of the handlebars (do not exceed maximum height) until you find your most comfortable riding position
- Good energy foods which don't take up much space are dates, figs, dried fruit and nuts
- Always thank people who make way for you
- Always take a few coins for emergencies
- Always allow extra time when planning a trip for delays caused by punctures, getting lost and so on
- If you forget your lock take your saddle and front wheel with you when you leave the bike. This is not recommended for any length of time and it is best to leave someone with the bikes if possible
- When riding in a group, plan the ride with the weakest person in mind. The fastest riders should go ahead and open gates for the rest of the group, shutting them afterwards, thus balancing out the difference in strength

Upper Littleton
Dundry Hill
Barrow Gurney

1 With back to The Angel PH L through Long Ashton

2 After 2½ miles, at T-J with B3130 L under bypass. Ignore R to Weston on A370, take next R up Barrow Court Lane (no through road). Follow road to end, ignoring Slade Lane to left

3 Where road ends, bear L towards conifer wood. Follow track uphill over X-roads of tracks ('Avon Cycleway Link'), keeping wood to your right (mud after rain) as far as gate

4 Through gate, SA for 30 yards through grass. R on track, continue in same direction through middle of field, roughly parallel with pine trees to the right. Join better track and go through grey metal gate

5 Pass barn on your left, 100 yards after road surface improves, L onto track. At T-j with tarmac R. At T-j with road L

6 At next T-j L. At A38 L then R 'Felton, Winford, Chew Magna'. After cattle grid 1st R, passing church on your left. Opposite church, fork R towards houses

8 Follow along edge of field on grassy surface to house with round oast house tower. Soon after surface improves near to oast tower, leave main track and fork L towards green pavilion. Keep to edge of field

9 At T-j of tracks R down broad track to road. At T-j with road L then 1st road R

10 At X-roads L past Five Gates 'Regil'. After about a mile, sharply back on yourself by metal gate (this section may be overgrown)

11 Pass a quarry on your left. At T-j with road L to the brow of hill then R. ***Not*** *Frog Lane but the stony track to the R of it*

12 At X-roads by Crown Hill Farm, SA onto track. At T-j of tracks after 400 yards near barn at bottom of hill turn R

13 At road L. At X-roads SA down Littleton Lane 'Upper Littleton ¼'

14 Ignore 1st R to Hazel End Farm after ½ mile. Shortly, take next R and climb steeply to top

15 At T-j with road L. Ignore 1st road to the right. After 200 yards as road swings L downhill bear R (in effect SA) through white gate by house into field

16 Keep next to wall/hedge on the right to go down steep muddy track to bottom

17 Emerge at road, SA onto stony track. Past engineering firm, R at T-j, which takes you to road

18 At road SA onto track opposite. Emerge at A38, L on pavement then 1st R along Freeman's Lane, past farm, through gate to rejoin original route

19 Go to gate at edge of conifer wood and down track with wood to your left

20 At X-roads of tracks at corner of wood, leave outward route. R through gateway. Follow edge of field through three gates (blue bridleway arrows) to road

21 SA, through gate, over grassy track down through field to gate. Take lane to road. R on road past Princes Motto PH. 1st road L very steeply uphill. At T-j after 200 yards bear L (in effect SA). At T-j after 1½ miles R on Weston Road to return to start

Ashton Court Estate
Homestead
CH
PH
P
Ashton Court
Coll
Bower Ashton
Sch
Country Club
Longwood Ho
Pill Grove
B 3128
Tyntesfield
Tyntesfield Plantn
Failand
Ashton Hill
A 370
Ashton Hill Plantn
Belmont Ho
Gable Fm
Long Ashton
Chapel
ROMAN SETTLEMENT
Depot
Yanley
Crem
Backwell Green
MS
Hospl
Inn
Cambridge Batch
Flax Bourton
Backwell Ho
Redwood Fm
Hospl
Bourton Combe
Mill
Barrow Wood
Motel
Barrow Court
Home Fm
B 3130
Barrow Gurney
Wks
Resr
Barrow Common
MP
Resrs
Barrow Hill
Mon
Highridge
Hyattswood Fm
Freemans Fm
Dundry
Castle Fm
Quarry (dis)
Elwell Fm
Potters Hill
Hanging Grove Fm
Upper Town
Felton
Lulsgate Bottom
Tumulus
Hospl
Bristol Airport
Felton Hill
Winford
Meade Fm
Tumuli
A 38
Upper Littleton
Cornerpool Fm
Glenmore Ho
Old Hill
Burial Chamber
Hunters Hall
Winford Manor
Kingdown
Butcombe Court
Littleton
Long Barrow
Myrtle House Fm
Hounsley Batch
Blackmoor
Redhill
Regilbury Court
Scars Fm
Rustin Fm
Pagans Hill
Lye Hole
The Oak
Regil
Regilbury Park Fm
Pigeon House Fm
Howgrove Fm
Walnut Tree Fm
1
2
3
4
5
6
7
8
9
10
11
12
13
14
15
16
17
18
19
20
21

A slice of Cheddar and a taste of the Mendips

The Carboniferous limestone of the Mendips provides a marked contrast to the surrounding countryside. The ride climbs the Mendips twice, offering panoramic views across the Bristol Channel and over the Somerset Levels and moors. There are two steep descents, one narrow and stony through woodland, the other somewhat broader, through forestry plantation. The top ridge may be muddy. The area is also popular with walkers and horses so show consideration, letting others pass and thanking them when they let you pass.

Start

The Edelweiss Restaurant, opposite the Cheddar Caves Information Booth at the lower end of Cheddar's main street

P The nearer the centre of Cheddar, the more expensive the car parks

Distance and grade

18 miles

Strenuous

Terrain

Two steep climbs from north and south of the Mendips. Forest tracks, open moorland, farm tracks

Nearest railway

Yatton, 6 miles from the route at Rowberrow

Places of interest

Cheddar Gorge *1*
The famous gorge is actually a collapsed cavern and runs for approximately one mile to the north-east of the village. The thickly wooded slopes and cliffs rise up to 1500 feet above the roadway. Much of the area is owned by the National Trust. Roman coins and remains of prehistoric man have been found in the caves in the gorge, some of which are open to the public.

Burrington Combe *6*
Another gorge, less spectacular than Cheddar. Augustus Toplady (1740-78) wrote the lines of the famous hymn 'Rock of ages cleft for me' while sheltering from a storm here.

Cheddar
King Down Farm
Beacon B

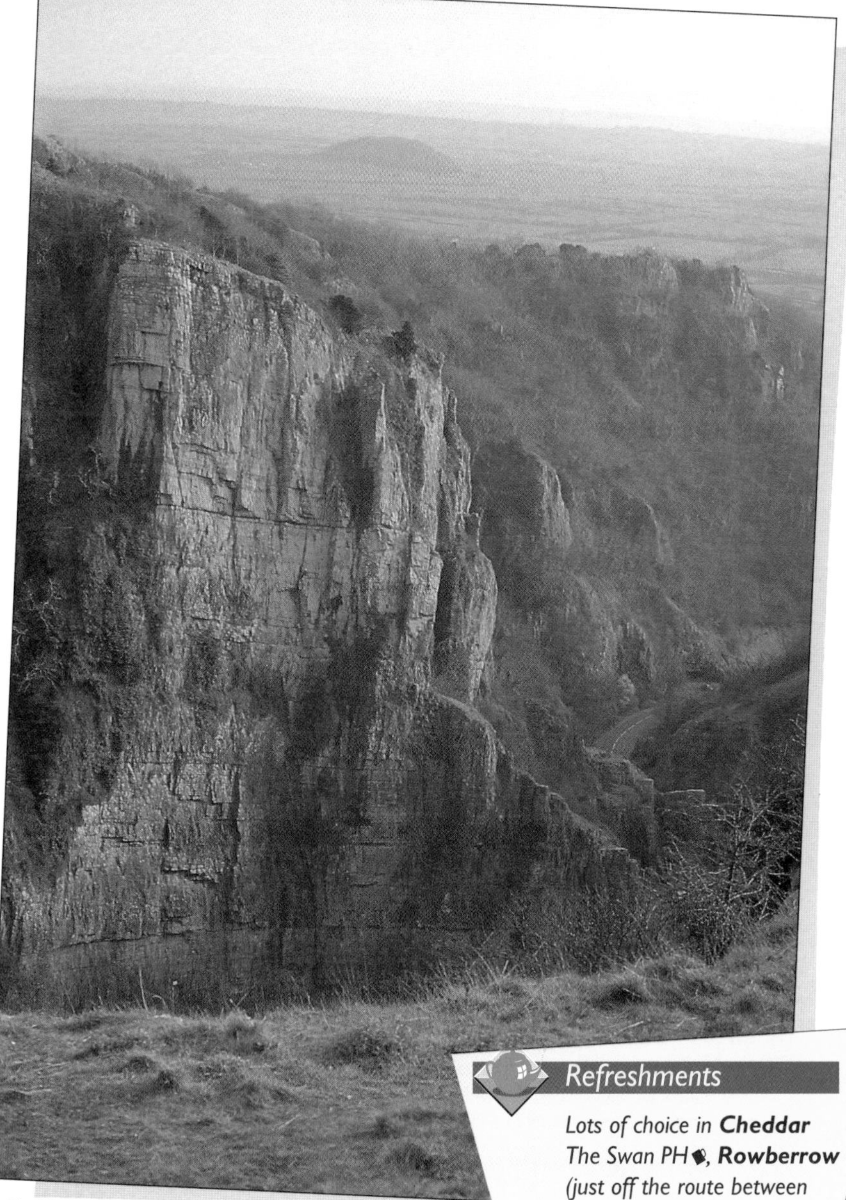

▲ *Cheddar Gorge*

Refreshments

Lots of choice in ***Cheddar***
The Swan PH, ***Rowberrow***
(just off the route between instructions 7 and 8)

Read's Cavern

1 From the Edelweiss Restaurant take the minor road out of Cheddar (to the left of St Andrews Road)

2 Pass Cheddar driving range on your left. At T-j L for 300 yards as far as signpost for Hilltops B&B. L then R, leaving Bradley Cottage on your left

3 Follow this grassy track towards copse, following blue arrows and signs for Daycott. Continue uphill through gate with two large wooden posts. Climb steeply on narrow stony track then more gently on broad farm track through several gates, eventually descending to the road

4 At X-roads with road (B3135) SA 'Compton Martin, Harptree'. After 1 mile 1st road L 'Charterhouse'. At X-roads near to Charterhouse church SA, then after ½ mile 1st L on bridleway towards masts

5 Keep to left of mast. At trig point continue in same direction towards top corner of plantation. At T-j of bridleways R then L to wood. There will be muddy stretches at all times of the year on the 2 mile section between the masts and the start of the wood. These will be at their worst from winter to late spring. The two alternatives are: drop down on the road through Burrington Combe then cut southwest to rejoin the route beneath Dolebury Warren **or**, *for a shorter ride, follow the road from the X-roads at Charterhouse to Tynings Farm and rejoin the route at instruction 10*

6 Straight descent through wood to gap between poles. After 50 yards, at X-roads of tracks L on good stony track through woodland

7 After a mile, in a small clearing with a green gate ahead and left of you turn L, passing a field, then stables on your right. (Keep a sharp eye out for this instruction)

8 Pass the pink, white and cream houses on your left, keeping to unmetalled track. At X-roads of bridleways SA, following blue arrow signs for Cheddar

9 Cross stream to your left and join forestry track coming up from the left. At X-roads of tracks SA to Tyning's Farm. Through farm to road

10 At road SA, with wall on your right. After 300 yards, as road bends R, SA 'Road unsuitable for motor vehicles'

11 Where this bears L into quarry SA down steep bridlepath into Cheddar. In open field take the broad track to the L and follow main track as it bends round to T-j with road

12 R on road (Hannay Road) then 1st L (Kent Street) to return to start

Lower Langford
Langford Court
Langford Green
Bourne
dismtd rly
Blagdon Lake
Rickford
Ford
Coombe Lodge (Coll)
Upper Langford
A 368
Link
Burrington
Blagdon
Nature Reserve
Fort
Mendip Lodge Wood
Settlement
Aveline's Hole
Burrington Ham
Fuller's Hay
Coll
Inn
Cemy
Dolebury Warren
Rowberrow
Warren Ho
Cavern
Rowberrow Warren
Read's Cavern
Rod's Pot
Goatchurch Cavern
Burrington Combe
Nature Reserve
Ellick Fm
Blagdon Hill Fm
Leaze Fm
M
E
N
D
Black Down
Beacon Batch
325
B 3134
Middle Ellick Fm
West Mendip Way
Tumulus
Tumuli
Settlements
Paywell Fm
Ubley Fm
Longbottom Fm
Tyning's Fm
Earthwork
312
299
Cave
Gorsey Bigbury Henge
Lower Fm
Roman Fort
Ashridge Fm
Manor Fm
Charterhouse
Nature Reserve
Long Wood
Ubley Warren Fm
The Perch
Piney Sleight Fm
Velvet Bottom
Warren Fm
Piney Sleight
Black Rock
MENDIP FOREST
Cheddar Gorge
Nature Trail
Cairn
King Down Fm
Rifle Range
Mus
Caves
Cheddar Cliffs
Tower
Wellington Fm
Yoxter Fm
Cheddar
Totty Pot Cave
Danger Area
B 3135
Bradley Cross
Palace (rems of)
Sch
Hythe
Nyland Manor
Halfway Fm
Carscliff Fm
Cheddar Head Fm
Prid Fm
Bristol Plain Fm
Batcombe Fm
A 371
Cheddar Moor
West Mendip Way
Settlement
Westbury Beacon
Draycott
Big Stoke
Long Barrow
Resr
Decoy Pool Fm
Court Fm
Nyland
Nyland Hill
Honeyhurst Fm
Rodney Stoke
Moor
Cemy
1
2
3
4
5
6
7
8
9
10
11
12

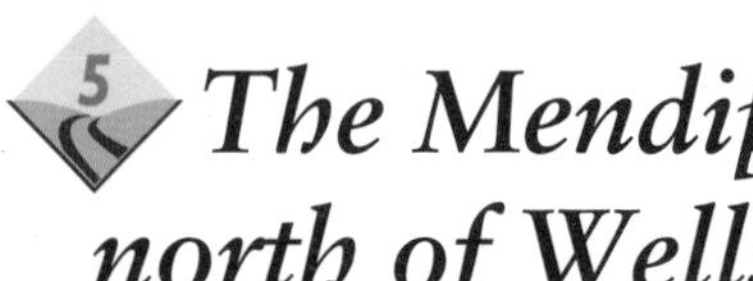

The Mendips north of Wells

The route for this energetic ride at the eastern end of the Mendips starts from the historic town of Wells and passes through the equally famous Wookey Hole. After a stiff road climb, you reach a ridge which provides panoramic views. A fast descent, part on-road, part off-road and semi-technical, leaves you at the start of the second climb, this time off-road. When you regain the ridge there is a short road section on quiet lanes before a last, lovely descent through Dinder Wood back to Wells.

There is a short section on a footpath across a field which saves you dropping down into and climbing back up from Wells and also avoids the busy A39. You must get off your bike and walk this quarter-mile section.

Start

Centre of Wells

P Follow signs from the centre of Wells

Distance and grade

16 miles

 Strenuous

Terrain

Two steep climbs up onto the Mendips, one on-road and one off-road. Farm tracks, woodland tracks

Nearest railway

Castle Cary, 10 miles southeast of Wells or Highbridge, 12 miles west of Wells

Off-road riding tips

- If using a jet spray to clean your bike, do not aim the hose directly at the hubs or bottom bracket but clean these parts from above
- Lubricate your bike after washing it or after a very wet ride, paying particular attention to the chain

Wells

Wookey Hole

Rookham

W

Places of interest

Wells *1*

Situated at the foot of the Mendip Hills, Wells is one of the smallest cathedral cities in England. Apart from its spectacular West Front the cathedral is worth a visit to see the 14th-century astronomical clock and the chapter house.

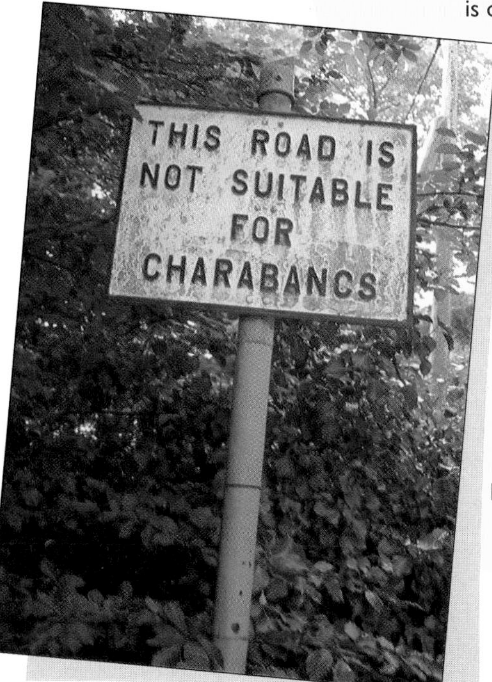

Wookey Hole *3*

Famous caverns worn away over thousands of years by the River Axe which can be heard rushing far below deep into the caves. There are no spectacular rock formations but the caverns are immense and there are relics of pre-historic man. Nearby is a mill dating back to the 17th century, that still produces hand-made paper.

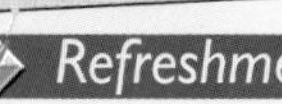

Refreshments

Plenty of choice in ***Wells and Wookey Hole***
Hunters Lodge Inn, ***Priddy*** *(1 mile north of the route at instruction 6)*
Slab House Inn, ***on the B3139*** *at instruction 13*

ydon

East Horrington

1 Head out of town on the A371 Cheddar road

2 Just past the Blue School, at the mini-roundabout, R on to Wookey Hole Road

3 Go through Wookey Hole, bearing R at a fork 'Single Track Road'

4 After a steep climb, as the road flattens out, 100 yards after passing a white house with a conservatory on your left, turn R on a track 'Ebbor Grove, Dursdon Drove'

5 Follow this track in the same direction for 2½ miles. It changes surface several times from farmtrack to grassy track and everything in between. 'No Cycling' signs will tell you where you must not ride. The surface eventually turns to tarmac and brings you to a T-j with the road

6 R steeply downhill, but do not lose all your height. After about ½ mile, as views start to open up on your right, opposite a sort of lay-by with gates on your right, turn L up a track past Ivy Cottage 'Bridleway'

7 Shortly, fork R down a narrow track. Although this track seems unlikely, it ***is*** *a bridleway. A semi-technical descent through a mossy sunken lane brings you to road*

(This adventurous track can at times be overgrown, muddy, rutted, stony, unrideable. If you wish to avoid this section, follow the road down, taking 1st L turn, rejoining route at second part of instruction 8)

8 At the road L. After 50 yards L again, then at a T-j L a 3rd time

9 On a sharp RH bend L by two metal garage doors

10 After 60 yards leave main track to go R over a stile. This ¼-mile section is a ***footpath****, so* ***walk*** *the bike diagonally L to the top LH corner of the field by a white house and a stone-built house*

11 Leave the field and turn L up track, following blue arrows and climbing steeply. Turn R on tarmac at the top

12 At X-roads with road SA 'Lower Haydon Farm'

13 Follow instructions carefully as there are few signposts on this road section: at T-j L then 1st R. At next T-j R, then at X-roads L 'Chilcote, Dinder'

14 At T-j R by The Beeches house. Pass the manor house and take the next R

15 Ignore track to right over cattle grid. Follow tarmac to gate. **Do not** *follow main track to left, but follow the hedge-row to your right, on firm grass*

16 Follow the track in this direction, bearing R when necessary, until the field narrows between woodland

17 Steeply down through woodland, through gate and fork L. At T-j with the A371 R (use pavement with discretion to avoid the main road). Shortly after the Fountain Inn turn L to go past the cathedral and return to the start

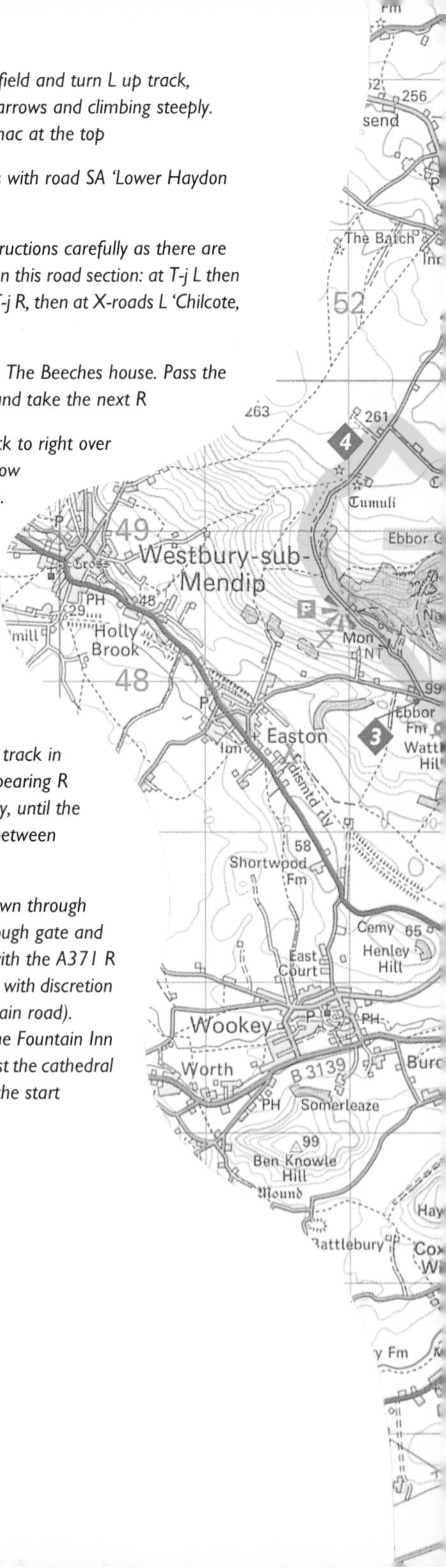

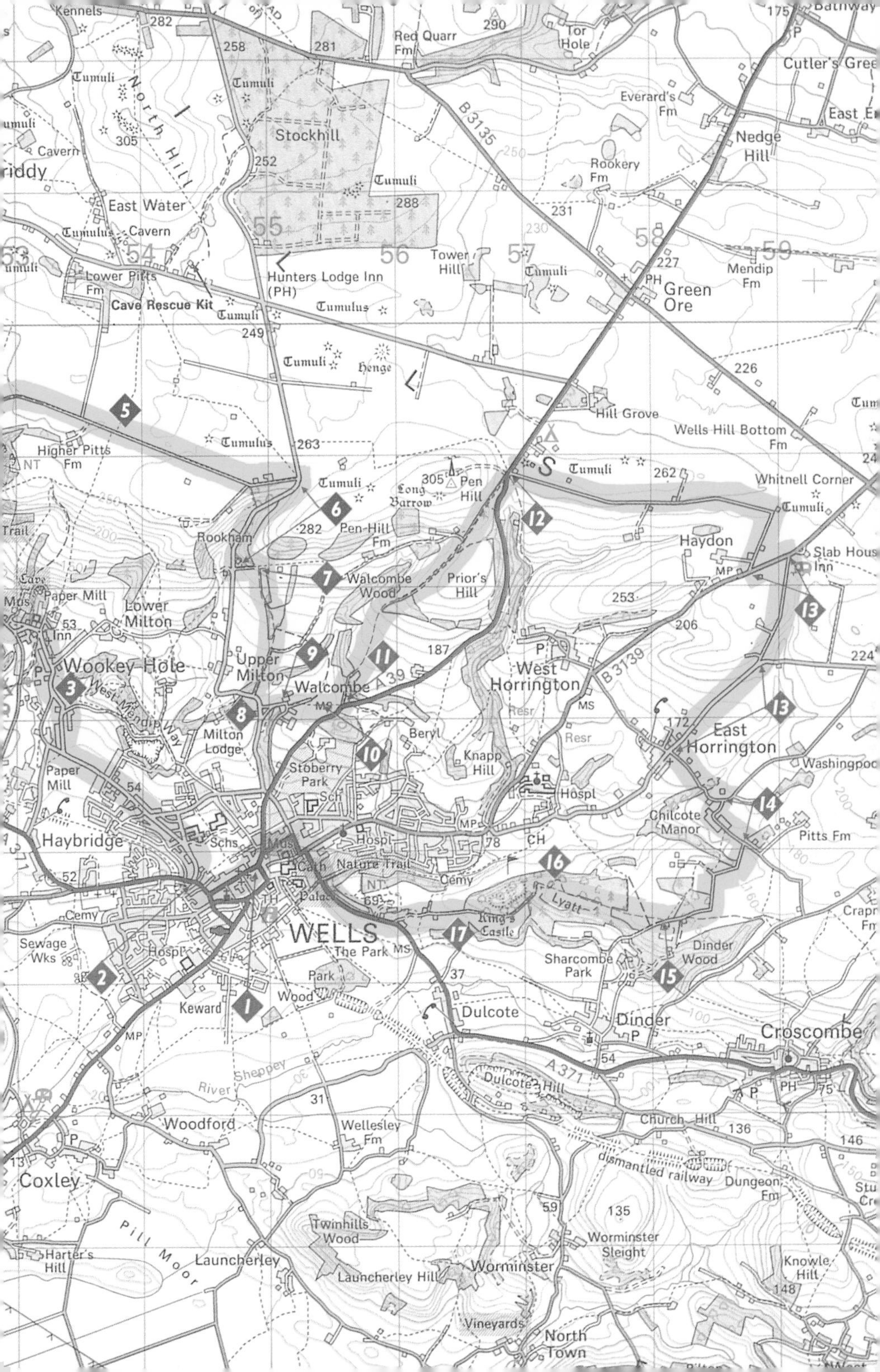
Stockhill
North Hill
East Water
Hunters Lodge Inn (PH)
Cave Rescue Kit
Lower Pitts Fm
Higher Pitts Fm
Green Ore
Rookery Fm
Everard's Fm
Nedge Hill
Mendip Fm
Tower Hill
Hill Grove
Wells Hill Bottom Fm
Whitnell Corner
Pen Hill
Long Barrow
Pen Hill Fm
Rookham
Walcombe Wood
Prior's Hill
Haydon
Slab House Inn
Paper Mill
Lower Milton
Wookey Hole
West Mendip Way
Upper Milton
Walcombe
Milton Lodge
West Horrington
East Horrington
Washingpool
Stoberry Park
Knapp Hill
Beryl
Chilcote Manor
Pitts Fm
Haybridge
WELLS
Nature Trail
King's Castle
Lyatt
Sharcombe Park
Dinder Wood
Dinder
Croscombe
The Park
Keward
Dulcote
Dulcote Hill
Church Hill
Dungeon Fm
Woodford
Wellesley Fm
River Sheppey
Coxley
Pill Moor
Harter's Hill
Launcherley
Launcherley Hill
Twinhills Wood
Worminster
Worminster Sleight
Vineyards
North Town
Knowle Hill
dismantled railway
Sewage Wks
B 3135
B 3139
A 39
A 371
1
2
3
5
6
7
8
9
10
11
12
13
14
15
16
17

High ridges between three Exmoor villages

Exmoor has a high density of bridleways, offering superb riding almost wherever you choose. This cycle ride links together three of the most picturesque villages on the moor via roads and tracks that are almost all passable year-round. The views are spectacular, as might be expected from a ride with so much climbing. Good refeshment stops are an added delight.

Start

Exford

P Follow signs in Exford

Distance and grade

18 miles

Strenuous

Terrain

Climbs out of each village: from Exford a steady road climb; from Withypool a very steep road climb and from Winsford a steep climb off-road past Kemps Farm. Two rough sections, one northwest of Withypool, the other near Knaplock; otherwise all year round tracks

Nearest railway

Tiverton Parkway, 25 miles

Refreshments

Royal Oak PH, **Withypool**
Royal Oak PH, **Winsford**
White Horse, Crown PH, **Exford**

Off-road riding tips

- The deepest part of a puddle on a farm track is usually where the vehicles' wheels go, so try the higher ground in the middle

Exford

Withypool

Comer's Cross

Places of interest

Exford *1*

This is the most important stag hunting centre on Exmoor and is the base for the Devon and Somerset Stag Hounds.

Withypool *8*

This village has one of the two legal commons existing in the Exmoor National Park. South of the village at Withypool Hill there is a stone circle among neolithic burial mounds.

▲ *Exmoor*

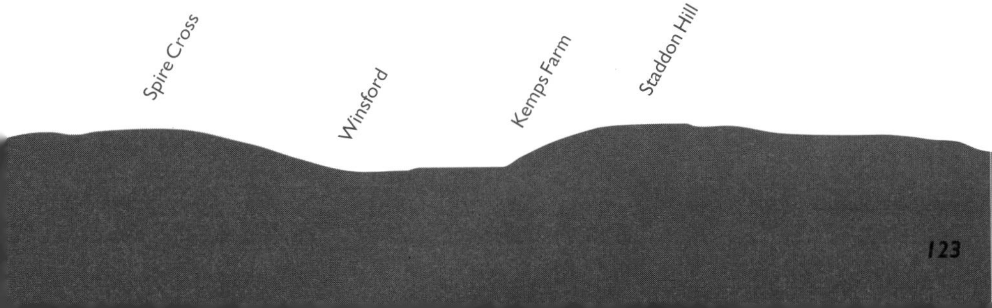

Spire Cross
Winsford
Kemps Farm
Staddon Hill

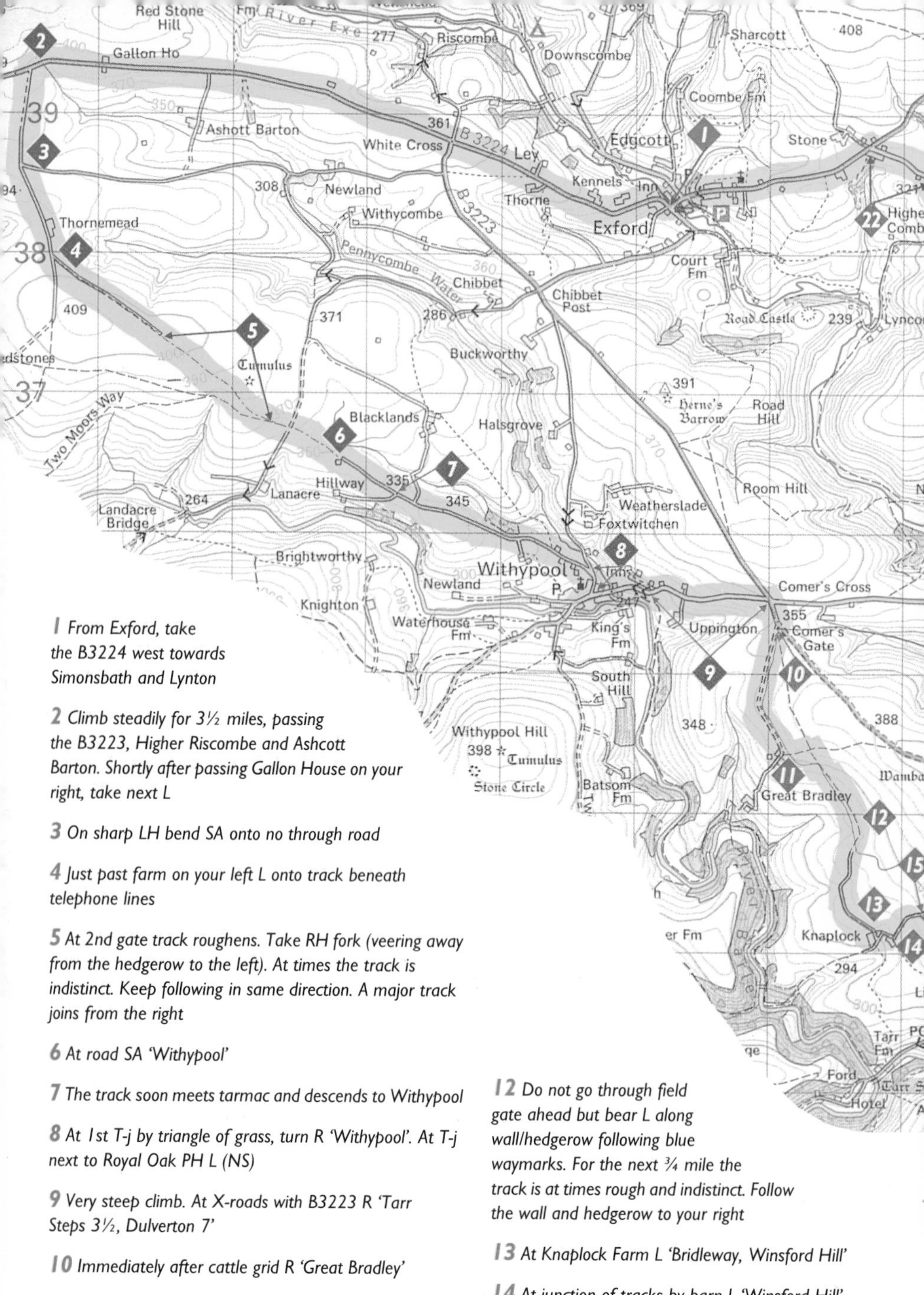

1 From Exford, take the B3224 west towards Simonsbath and Lynton

2 Climb steadily for 3½ miles, passing the B3223, Higher Riscombe and Ashcott Barton. Shortly after passing Gallon House on your right, take next L

3 On sharp LH bend SA onto no through road

4 Just past farm on your left L onto track beneath telephone lines

5 At 2nd gate track roughens. Take RH fork (veering away from the hedgerow to the left). At times the track is indistinct. Keep following in same direction. A major track joins from the right

6 At road SA 'Withypool'

7 The track soon meets tarmac and descends to Withypool

8 At 1st T-j by triangle of grass, turn R 'Withypool'. At T-j next to Royal Oak PH L (NS)

9 Very steep climb. At X-roads with B3223 R 'Tarr Steps 3½, Dulverton 7'

10 Immediately after cattle grid R 'Great Bradley'

11 As track bears sharply R downhill over cattle grid turn L, uphill, at T-j of tracks, then bear R 'Tarr Steps via Knaplock'

12 Do not go through field gate ahead but bear L along wall/hedgerow following blue waymarks. For the next ¾ mile the track is at times rough and indistinct. Follow the wall and hedgerow to your right

13 At Knaplock Farm L 'Bridleway, Winsford Hill'

14 At junction of tracks by barn L 'Winsford Hill'

15 Bear R, staying on major track 'Winsford via Winsford Hill'

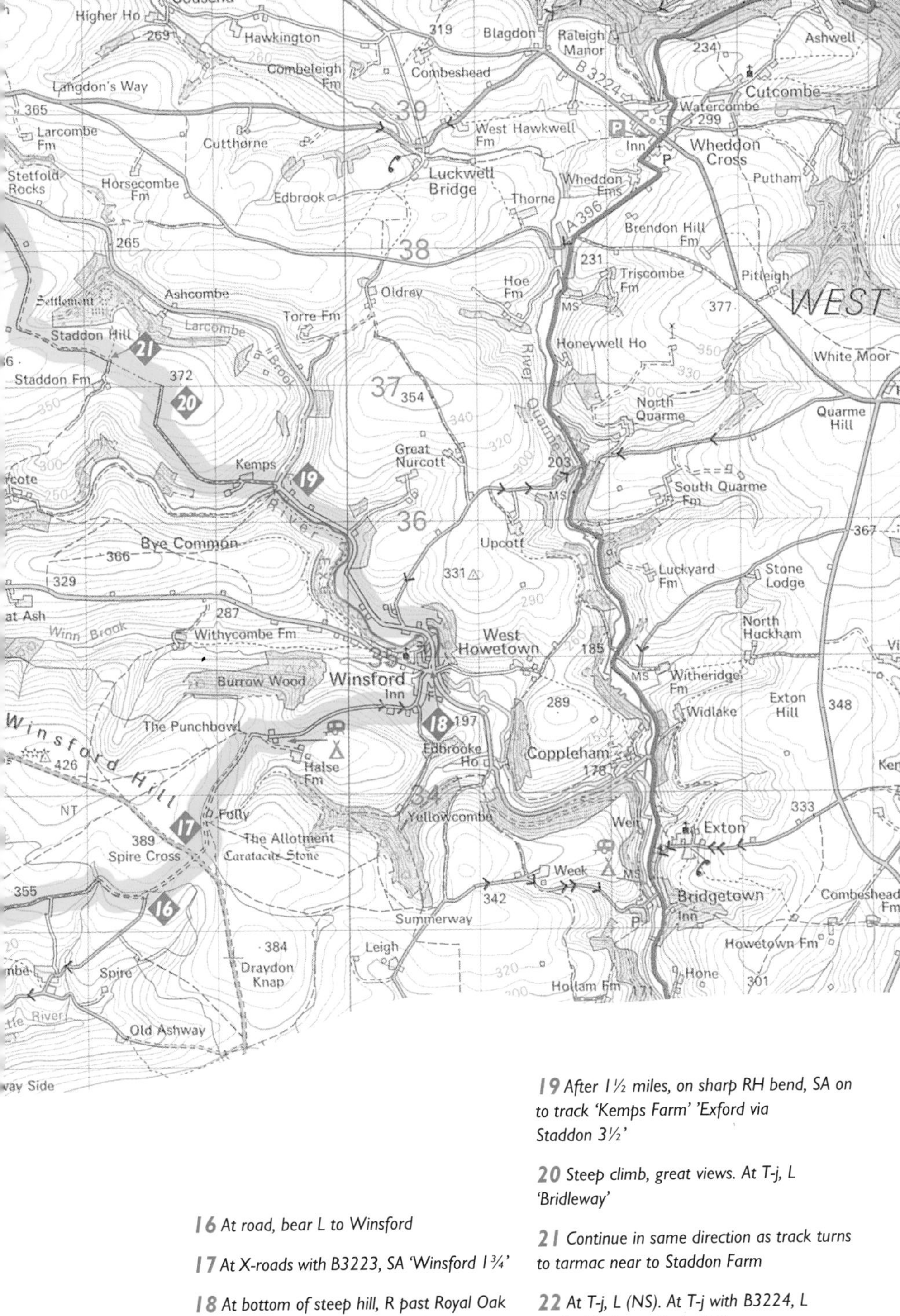

16 At road, bear L to Winsford

17 At X-roads with B3223, SA 'Winsford 1¾'

18 At bottom of steep hill, R past Royal Oak PH, then L at T-j 'Exford, Simonsbath'

19 After 1½ miles, on sharp RH bend, SA on to track 'Kemps Farm' 'Exford via Staddon 3½'

20 Steep climb, great views. At T-j, L 'Bridleway'

21 Continue in same direction as track turns to tarmac near to Staddon Farm

22 At T-j, L (NS). At T-j with B3224, L 'Exford 1, Simonsbath 6½'

Around Wimbleball Lake, Exmoor

The two loops of this ride to the south of the Brendon Hills give you the option of three rides of different lengths.

The southern loop (10 miles) takes the track east from the dam through woods to the B3190, cuts back west on road to the car park at Haddon Hill, then descends on an amazing, steep, sunken track that is at times overgrown, muddy, rutted, stony or unrideable but always beautiful and a real adventure. If this sounds a bit rough, then there is an alternative descent by road to the ford at Bury to rejoin the route. The next part is the best of the whole trip as the route follows the River Haddeo along Hartford Bottom, then on Lady Harriet's Drive on broad tracks back to the dam beneath the lake. A very steep climb takes you up on to the dam and back to the car park.

The northern and easier loop (7 miles) follows the edge of Wimbleball Lake before climbing 250 feet to the remains of St James Church on Upton Hill. Having descended to Upton, the ride retraces the outward route of the southern loop on the track that runs westwards along the bottom edge of the lake to cross the dam and return to the car park. There are fine views all around this loop.

Start

Wimbleball Lake Water Park, 4 miles south of the B3224 between Bishops Lydeard and Wheddon Cross. Alternatively, Haddon Hill car park on the B3190 east of Dulverton

P As above

Distance and grade

7 and 10 miles (two loops total 17 miles)

(1) to (5) according to which loops are chosen

Terrain

From easy tracks to technical descents. One short, very steep climb on road just south of the dam and a more gentle one from the north end of the lake up to Upton Farm, part on-road, part off-road

Nearest railway

Tiverton Parkway, 16 miles to the southeast

Higher Cowlings
Dam
Haddon Farm

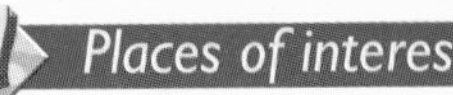

Places of interest

Wimbleball Lake Water Park *16*
374 acres of water and 500 acres of surrounding woodland and meadow. Tea rooms situated in the park.

Refreshments

Tea shop at the car park by the reservoir

▲ *Wimbleball Lake*

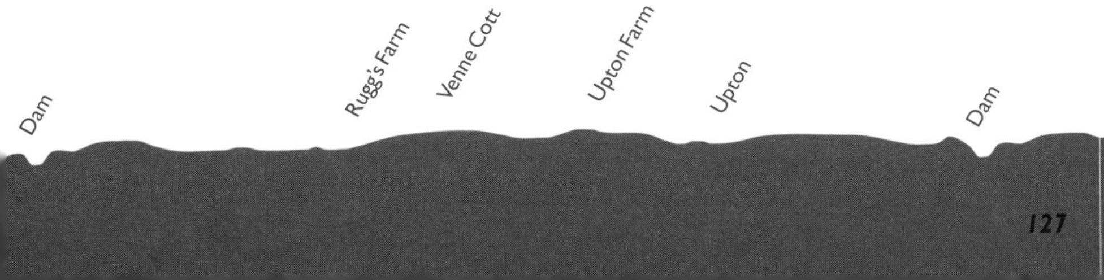

Dam
Rugg's Farm
Venne Cott
Upton Farm
Upton
Dam

Loop 1

1 Out of Wimbleball Lake Water Park and turn L

2 Shortly after reaching the brow of the hill, by triangle of grass, R uphill 'Hartford, Haddon Hill'

3 Keep bearing L towards dam. Cross bridge, L on Lady Harriet's Drive 'Upton 1¾'

4 1st L on Lady Harriet's Drive 'Upton 1½' (the track from Haddon Hill car park joins the route at this point)

5 Stay on main, lower track through woodland through several gates to road

6 At road R

7 After 1 mile, on sharp LH bend (Haddon Hill car park on right) SA on track just to the left of a white house. (If you do not fancy the steep, rough off-road descent, follow road to X-roads, turn R and rejoin route at ford)

8 At farm buildings by Haddon Farm bear L towards sunken grassy track. Good luck!

9 Follow track onto tarmac. At T-j with road, near telephone box, R

10 Through ford or over bridge. Bear R, past Old School House, down no through road

11 SA through white wooden gate, past lodge 'Bridleway to Hartford 2, Upton 4¾'

12 After 2 miles, at junction of tracks, L 'Upton 2½, Haddon Hill, Dam, avoiding houses'

13 After 300 yards R through wooden gate over bridge

14 Shortly after 2nd gate, fork R very steeply uphill

15 Cross bridge, L 'Brompton Regis 2¼' retrace route back to car park bearing L at T-j with road by triangle of grass then after ¾ mile R over cattle grid 'Wimbleball Park, Main Entrance'

Loop 2

16 From the information centre in the car park go straight downhill towards the lake on a grassy track by the hedgerow

17 Near the lake L, following signs for Bessom Bridge. At X-roads with tarmac lane SA passing a wooden hut on your right

18 At road R to cross bridge

19 1st R 'Upton 2½, Wiveliscombe 8½'

20 Climb steeply. Ignore 1st R to Lower Holworthy Farm. Take next R 'No Through Road'

21 At the T-j by the ruins of the church L

22 At T-j by Rainsbury House bear R downhill (in effect SA)

23 At T-j with B3190 R 'Bampton 6, Dulverton 6'

24 Just after white cottage on left, ignore footpath to the right, take next R through wide wooden gate L 'Hartford 2, Dam 1½'

25 At fork of tracks with the lake visible to the right, bear L on upper, more major track. Retracing route, at T-j R 'Wimbleball Dam ¼, Bury 2¾'

26 Over dam and L to return to water park

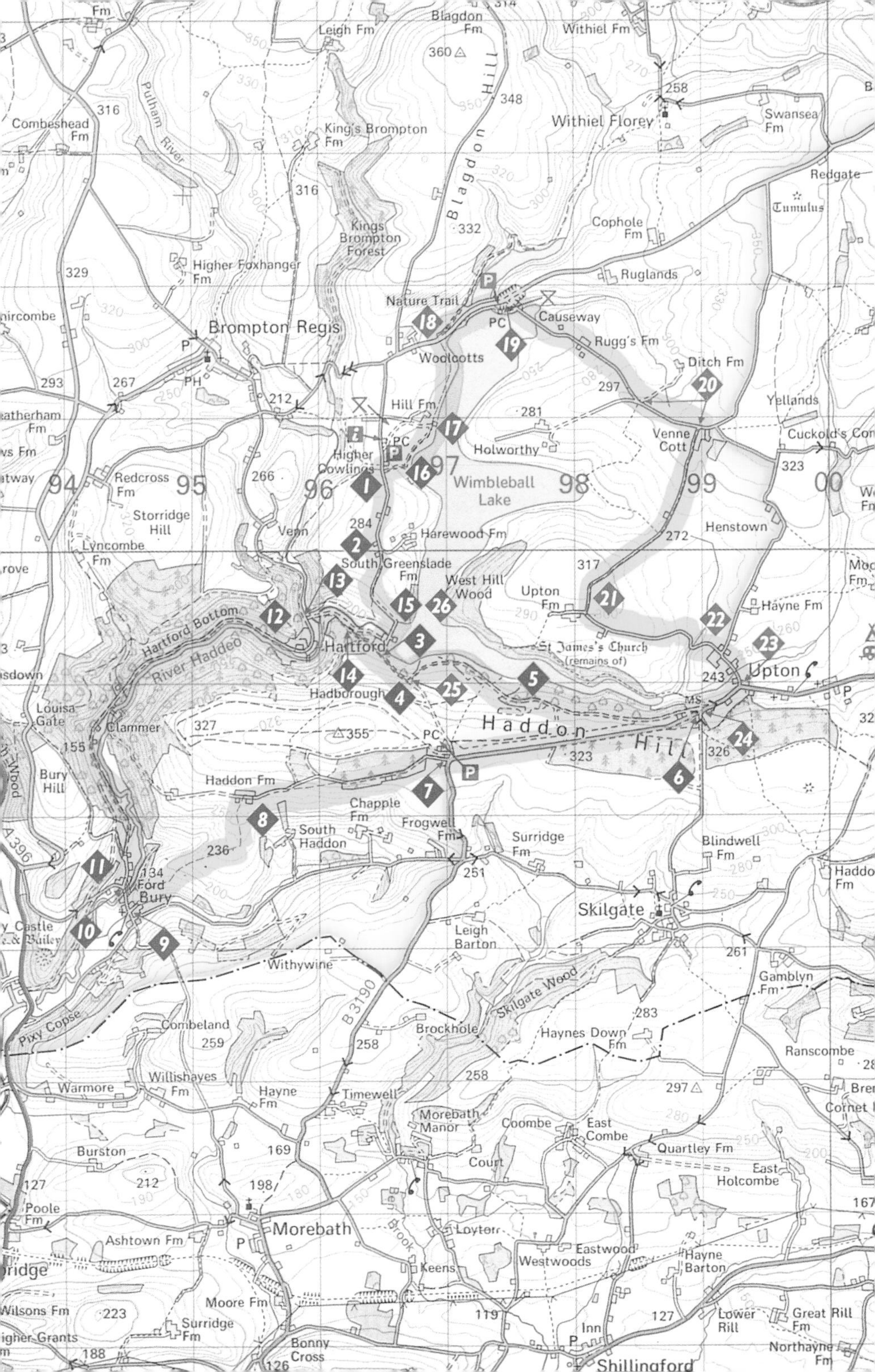

Brompton Regis
Wimbleball Lake
Haddon Hill
Hartford
Upton
Skilgate
Morebath
Bury
Withiel Florey
Kings Brompton Forest
Hartford Bottom
River Haddeo
Skilgate Wood
Pixy Copse
Nature Trail
St James's Church (remains of)

Chalk Ridges north of Mere

The ride is on the western edge of the chalklands that run from the Dorset coast to Swindon and beyond. The highest point of the ride is on White Sheet Hill (800 feet), from where there are superb views of Somerset. This is also the site of a Neolithic camp.

Start

Car park on the lane running east from the Red Lion Inn on the B3092 road (Mere to Maiden Bradley) towards White Sheet Hill

P As above

Distance and grade

15 miles

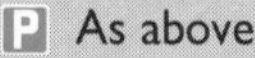 Moderate/strenuous

Terrain

Mainly broad chalk tracks and farm tracks. May be muddy after rain and in winter

Nearest railway

Gillingham, 7 miles South of White Sheet Hill

Off-road riding tips

- Alter your starting point to take account of the wind direction so that you are not cycling back into the wind when you are tired
- Discretion is the better part of valour – do not be persuaded to do something which you feel is way beyond your abilities
- If you come across a blocked right of way or one you feel is in a terrible state of repair report it to the Rights of Way Department at the County Council. The most effective means is to write a letter giving grid references

Kilmington

Norton Ferris

▲ *Steep climb from Rodmead farm*

Places of interest

Stourhead *3*

One of the earliest English Palladian mansions, Stourhead House was built for Sir Henry Hoare by Colen Campbell and completed in 1725. It is most famous for its grounds which take the form of an idealised Italian landscape and include a grotto, a Temple of Apollo and the Bristol Cross which was brought from Bristol in the 18th century. They were laid by Henry Hoare II and the architect Henry Flitcroft starting in 1744.

Refreshments

Red Lion PH, ***Kilmington***

Kingston Deverill

Monkton Deverill

Charnage Down

White Sheet Downs

1 L out of the car park down the hill to the B3092

2 At X-roads with B3092 SA onto track. The first ¼ mile is a bit rough. To avoid the worst of the mud and roughest of the tracks, turn R on the road for 1 mile and rejoin the route at instruction 7. Turn R off the B3092 at a triangle of grass with a Norton Ferris sign down a No Through Road

3 At X-roads at the end of Kilmington Common by red-brick house R then after ¼ mile at 2nd X-roads R again 'Kilmington'

4 At T-j by memorial stone L, then after ¼ mile, by a bench beneath a copper beech tree, R onto track

5 Gently downhill. Ignore field gates to the left. After ½ mile L on track (no gate) 'Byway'

6 Rough section. Ignore gateways to the right. After ½ mile, with better track ahead, 1st R onto track towards distinctive round hill

7 Gently downhill to road. R then L down no through road

8 200 yards past Elm Farm, on sharp RH bend, leave tarmac to go SA through gateway into field onto rough track running along LH field edge

9 Through gate into next field, through field and onto road

10 At road R towards Rodmead Farm and through farmyard. Through metal gate and bear L up steep chalk track with fine views opening up

11 ***Follow directions carefully!*** *As track levels, at junction of tracks near gate (blue arrows and 2-way 'Bridleway' signs) L through gate heading across open field to another gate slightly left of straight ahead (11 o'clock). Go through the 2nd gate and L gently downhill alongside fence for 300 yards until reaching a wicket gate with a blue bridleway sign. Turn R to contour along hillside towards the LH end of the wood*

12 Go through gate near end of wood and contour along hillside towards the fence on your right. Follow this to the end then bear down and across the field towards a bridlegate

13 Cross concrete track and through 2nd bridlegate then diagonally L across field to gate

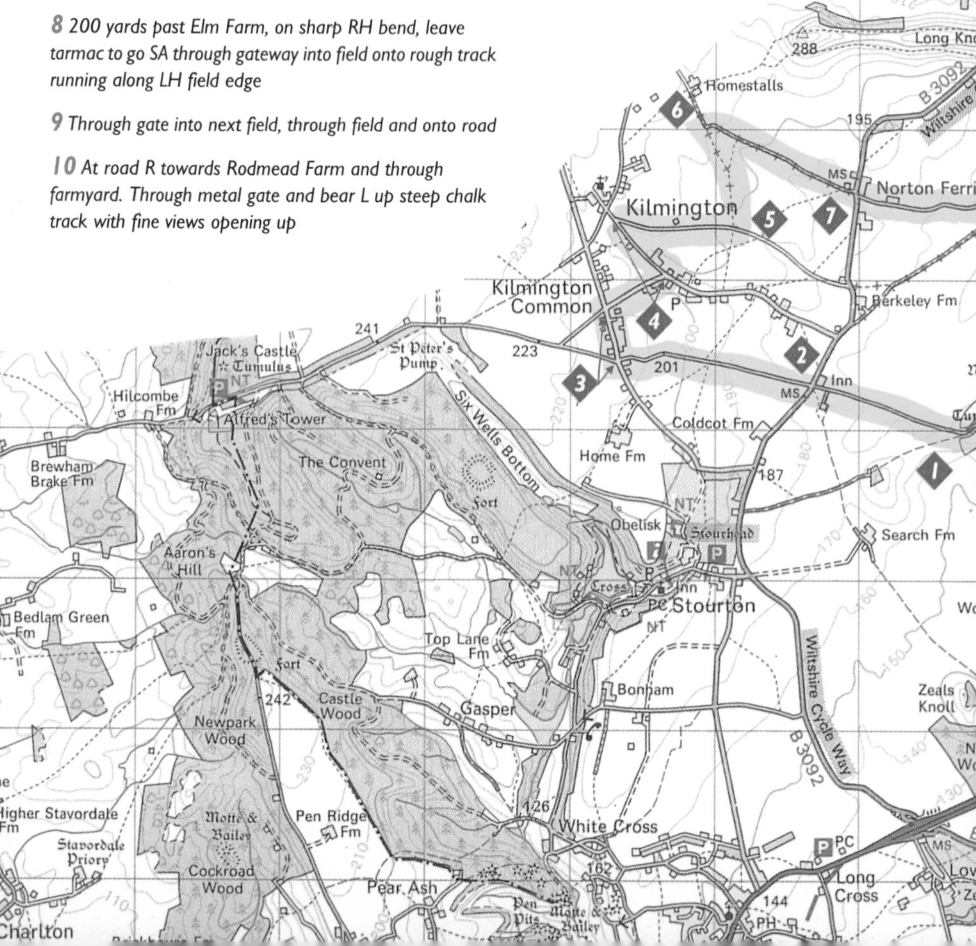

14 *At T-j with road by signs for Gliding Club and near a telegraph pole with lines from all directions, turn R through village*

15 *At T-j (with B3095) by the church bear L (in effect SA)*

16 *On reaching sign for Monkton Deverill 1st R '7.5 ton weight limit', then 1st R again by metal gate, up a tarmac lane*

17 *At metal gate SA into field, taking the lower track next to the hedge*

18 *Through two more gates, closely spaced, then* ***ignore*** *obvious track that climbs steeply to right and carry along grassy valley bottom, passing a hawthorn tree on your left, heading towards gate*

19 *Through gate and climb out of valley on obvious track to another gate*

20 *On track through middle of field to yet another gate, then along RH edge of field to T-j with major track, with the A303 in sight and earshot*

21 *Turn R and follow this track for about 4 miles, crossing the B3095 to White Sheet Hill. Follow main track back down to starting point and car park*

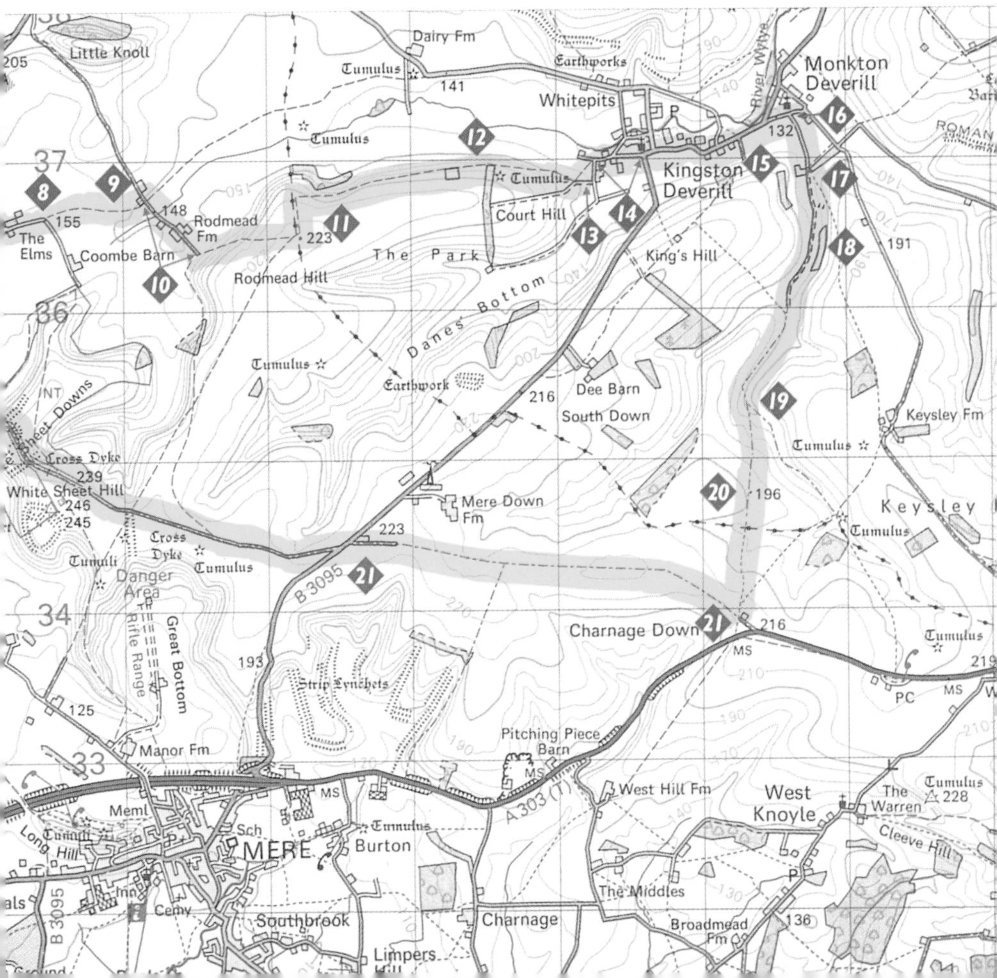

9 Ancient roads in Wiltshire

The route of this ridge ride through Wiltshire downland follows the old Salisbury to Exeter coach road outwards and returns on the Roman road that used to run from the Mendips to Old Sarum via Grovely Wood. There are fine views of rolling Wiltshire countryside at several points. The route is entirely off-road although some of the surfaces are as good as roads, particularly on the return half which is, consequently, much easier than the outward half.

Start

The Square, Wilton

P On side streets or on roads out of town

Distance and grade

25 miles

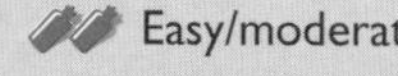

Easy/moderate

Terrain

Mainly good broad tracks on ridges through woodland or over chalk downland

Nearest railway

Salisbury, 4 miles east of Wilton

◄ Wilton House (see page 91)

Wilton

Crouch's Down

Stockton Earthworks

Off-road cycling tips

- If there is a grating or crunching noise when you spin the wheels, pedals or cranks replace the bearings before they damage more expensive parts
- If some vegetation gets stuck in your derailleur, remove it straightaway before it does any damage
- Anticipate hills by changing into the right gear before it gets tough
- Drink before you get thirsty and eat before you get hungry. Regular small amounts are better than a big lunch
- Leave no litter
- Make sure there is nothing loose and dangling (laces, daypack straps, pannier straps) which may get caught in the spokes, chain or pedals
- If there is any chance of cycling in twilight or darkness, take lights with you. As a precaution in winter, take a reflective belt and/or reflective strips for ankles and wrists – being visible is what matters most
- If carrying bikes on a car, stop regularly to check they are securely fixed
- When riding in a group ensure everyone has the equipment to mend a puncture (pump, tyre levers, puncture repair kit and/or spare inner tube). With four other tools: a reversible screwdriver, a small adjustable spanner, a set of appropriate allen keys and a chain link extractor, you have all you need. All this fits in a small pouch, worn around your waist or attached under the saddle

1 Take the A30 out of Wilton heading west towards Shaftesbury, passing the Italianate church on your left

2 At the Bell Inn R along Water Ditchampton 'Great Wishford'

3 Under the bridge and immediately L 'Hollows no through road'

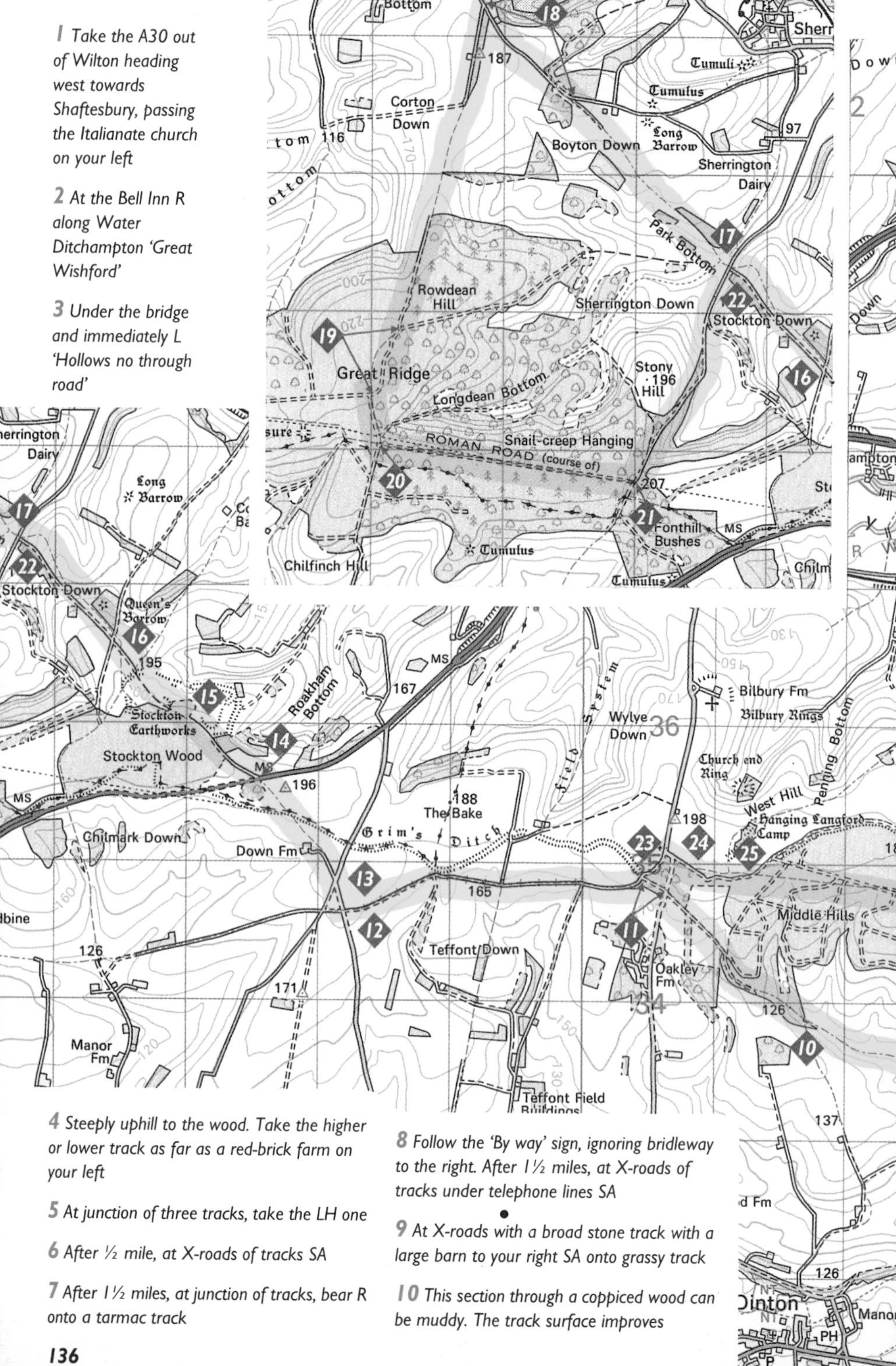

4 Steeply uphill to the wood. Take the higher or lower track as far as a red-brick farm on your left

5 At junction of three tracks, take the LH one

6 After ½ mile, at X-roads of tracks SA

7 After 1½ miles, at junction of tracks, bear R onto a tarmac track

8 Follow the 'By way' sign, ignoring bridleway to the right. After 1½ miles, at X-roads of tracks under telephone lines SA

9 At X-roads with a broad stone track with a large barn to your right SA onto grassy track

10 This section through a coppiced wood can be muddy. The track surface improves

11 *At the Wylye-Dinton road SA. Shortly after, at concrete track L 'Byway'*

12 *(For the next 3½ miles, as far as Queens Barrow X-roads, this section forms part of both the outward and return route) Follow the concrete track for 1½ miles*

13 *At X-roads with tarmac road R. After 100 yards, at X-roads SA towards the pink house'No MOD vehicles'*

14 *Through gate and wood to emerge at the busy A303 SA onto muddy track.*

15 *Emerge from woodland, carry on across grassland, bearing R (northwest), with Stockton earthworks to the right*

16 *At X-roads of tracks (Queens Barrow) SA through wide metal gate, keeping the wood on the right. Descend to road. (*Return trip rejoins route at this point)*

17 *At road L then R uphill on track*

18 *At metalled track L. Just before a collection of barns on the right turn L onto track between fence and trees*

19 *Once into a conifer forest with trees on both sides, ignore 1st left turn on stone track. After ¾ mile, shortly after sharp RH bend, next stone track L*

20 *Take 2nd L along well-made gravel track*

21 *After 1¼ miles, at T-j L steeply downhill. The surface improves and soon you rejoin the outward route (*)*

22 *Turn R uphill through gate. The byway bears L then rejoins the concrete track a little higher. Retrace your tracks from the outward leg for 3½ miles passing Queen's Barrow, Stockton earthworks and crossing the A303 (**take care**). At X-roads with road SA 'Teffont' then 1st L 'Byway' to rejoin the concrete track that leads to the Wylye–Dinton road*

23 *Do **not** turn R off this but follow it to the end as it turns to rough gravel to join the Wylye–Dinton road slightly north of the outward crossing*

24 *At road R, then L (in effect SA) on a sharp RH bend after 60 yards*

25 *At the Simplex barn bear R*

26 *After passing a farm on the right, take the 2nd R by a triangle of grass where the telephone lines cross from left to right to follow the ridge through magnificent beech trees, past the red-brick farm back into Wilton*

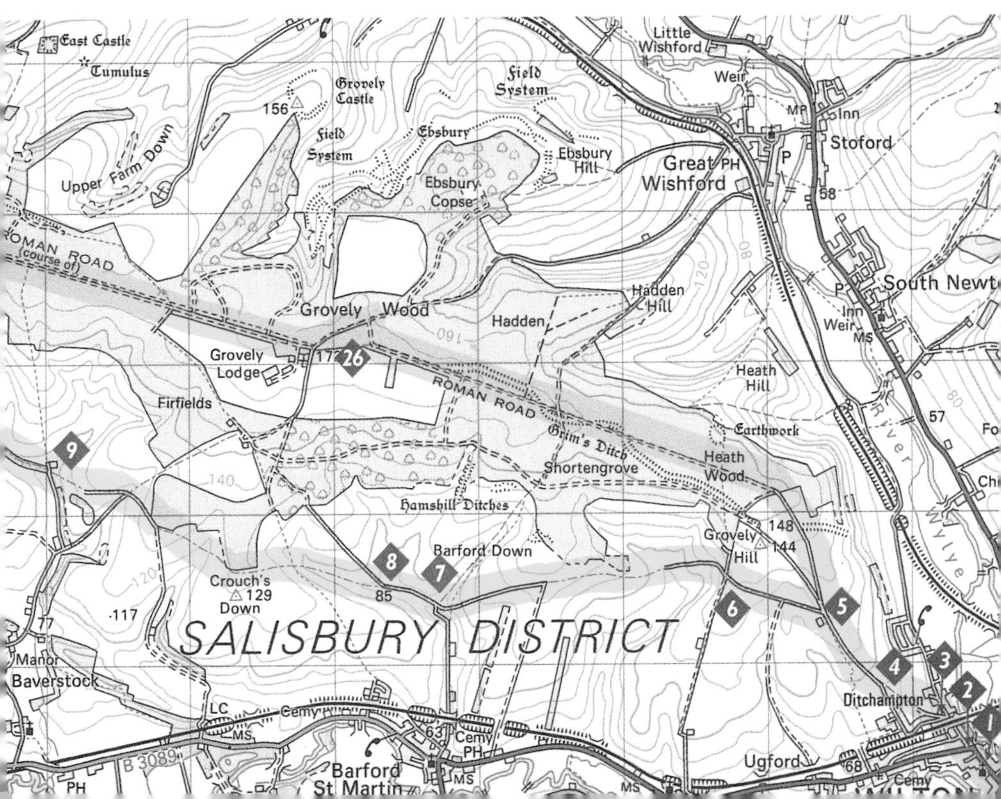

Ridge tracks and ox droves west of Wilton

Spread out fan-like to the west of Wilton are a series of valleys and ridges that provide some very enjoyable on-road and off-road cycling. The on-road rides tend to follow the valleys and the off-road, the ridges. This ride crosses the River Nadder to the south of Wilton and climbs past Hunt's Down through woodland to the main east-west ridge. A superb, easy track heads west between hedgerows, with views alternating to the north and south. The route drops to Alvediston, then climbs steeply to the parallel ridge to the south, the Ox Drove, which is rougher track than the earlier ridge. A gentle 250-foot descent to Broad Chalke via Church Bottom leaves you with one final climb past Flamstone Farm back to the first ridge and an exhilarating descent back to Wilton.

Start

The Square, Wilton

P On various side roads off the main roads out of town

Distance and grade

25 miles

Moderate

Terrain

Excellent off-road riding on the ridge between Hunt's Down, west–southwest to Middle Down, a steep descent and climb via Alvediston to reach the Ox Drove ridge further south, which is rougher and may be muddy. A final steep climb on sealed surface past Flamstone Farm to regain first ridge

Nearest railway

Salisbury, 3 miles east of Wilton

Refreshments

*Crown Inn PH, **Alvediston***
*Horseshoe PH, **Ebbesbourne Wake** (1 mile east of the route at Alvediston)*
*Queens Head PH, **Broad Chalke***
*White Hart PH, **Bishopstone***

Wilton
Hunt's Down
Fovant Hill
Middle Down
Alvedisto

Off-road riding tips

- Do not expect your friendly bike shop to repair your bike at a moment's notice, particularly on a Friday in summer!
- Clean your bike of mud before expecting a mechanic to work on it
- When coming up behind a horse, give the rider plenty of warning with a big 'Hallooo'
- Leave a reasonable distance between you and the rider in front: you never know what obstacles he/she may come across
- Let someone know where you are going, particularly if it is winter and you are going to a remote area.
- The same off-road route can take much longer after rain or in the winter when tracks are softer, so plan accordingly
- If using British Rail, always phone in advance to check what the regulations are for the service you wish to use and if a reservation is required
- Plan a ride with the weakest person in mind
- To get an early start, prepare your equipment and bike the night before
- Make yourself a checklist which you can use whenever you go off on a ride, amending it for weekends away or winter riding
- Aside from the whole bike the most likely things to be stolen are: bicycle computer, panniers, lights, pump, saddle. If you can't be bothered to take the whole lot, at least take your wallet/purse and keys

Cow Down Hill
Ox Drove Ridge
Broad Chalke
Stoke Farthing
Flamstone Farm

1 From the traffic lights in the square in Wilton, take South Street 'Bishopstone 4, Broad Chalke 6'

2 1st R after the bridge 'Burcombe'

3 Pass a housing estate on left, take track L opposite house on the right and 'No entry' sign.
The track is signposted 'Public right of way'

4 Steady climb to T-j at start of wood. Turn R by line of beech trees. Remember this point for return trip

5 Carry on climbing through woodland ignoring turnings until emerging onto ridge at edge of
wood at major X-roads of tracks by a triangle of grass. Turn R. Remember this point for return trip

6 At T-j with more major track after 2 miles bear L, then shortly, as main track swings left bear R (in effect SA) onto grassy track. At X-roads with tarmac after 3 miles SA

7 After a further 2½ miles, at 2nd tarmac road, L to descend to Alvediston

8 At X-roads in Alvediston R 'Berwick St John, Shaftesbury' then 1st L up tarmac lane/track

9 430 feet climb, steep at the end. At X-roads of tracks on the ridge with a barn ahead turn L

10 Follow the ridge on track, then on tarmac for 1 mile 'Handley'

11 At T-j SA onto track 'Byway to drove road'

12 At next road SA onto track 'Byway'

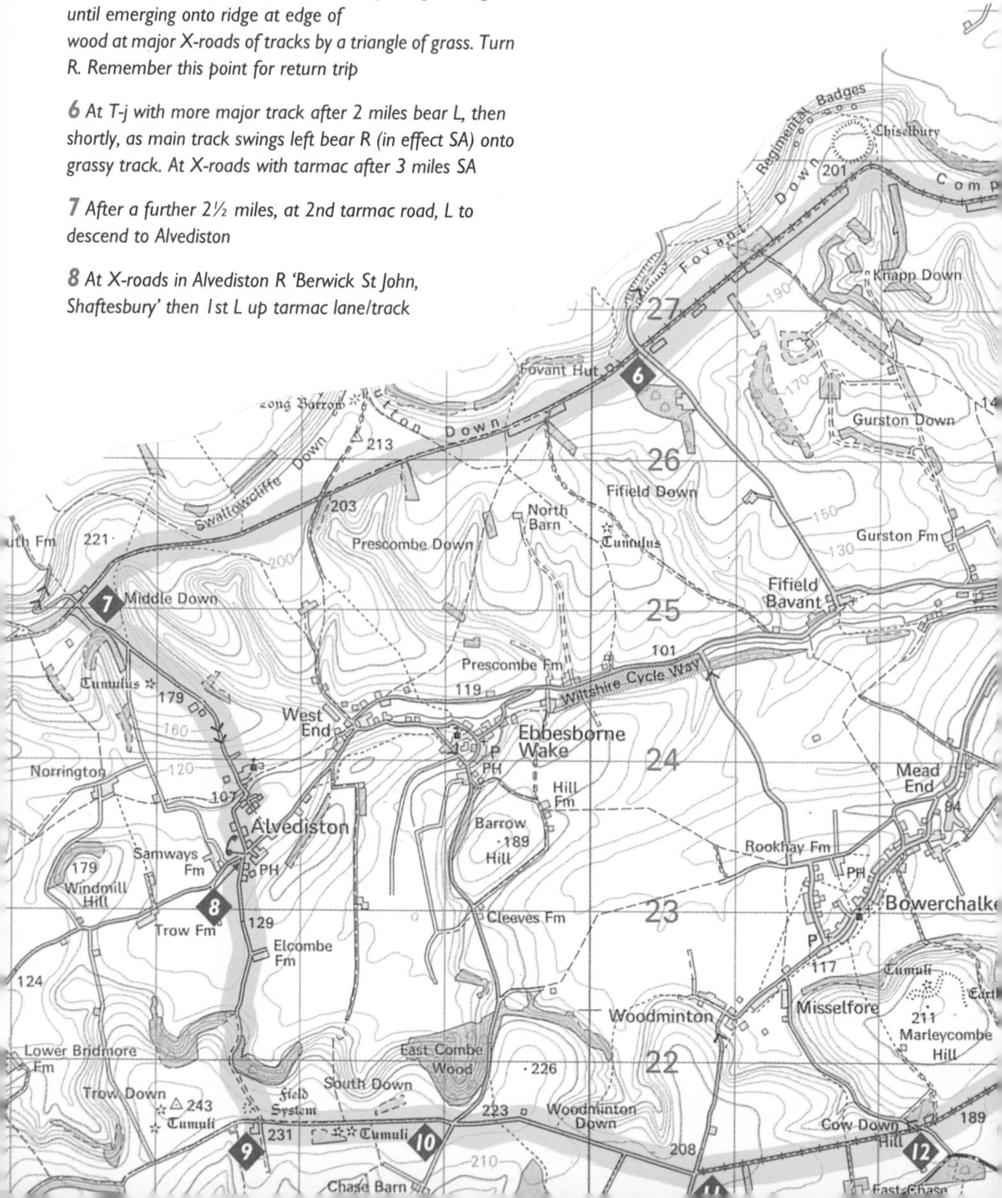

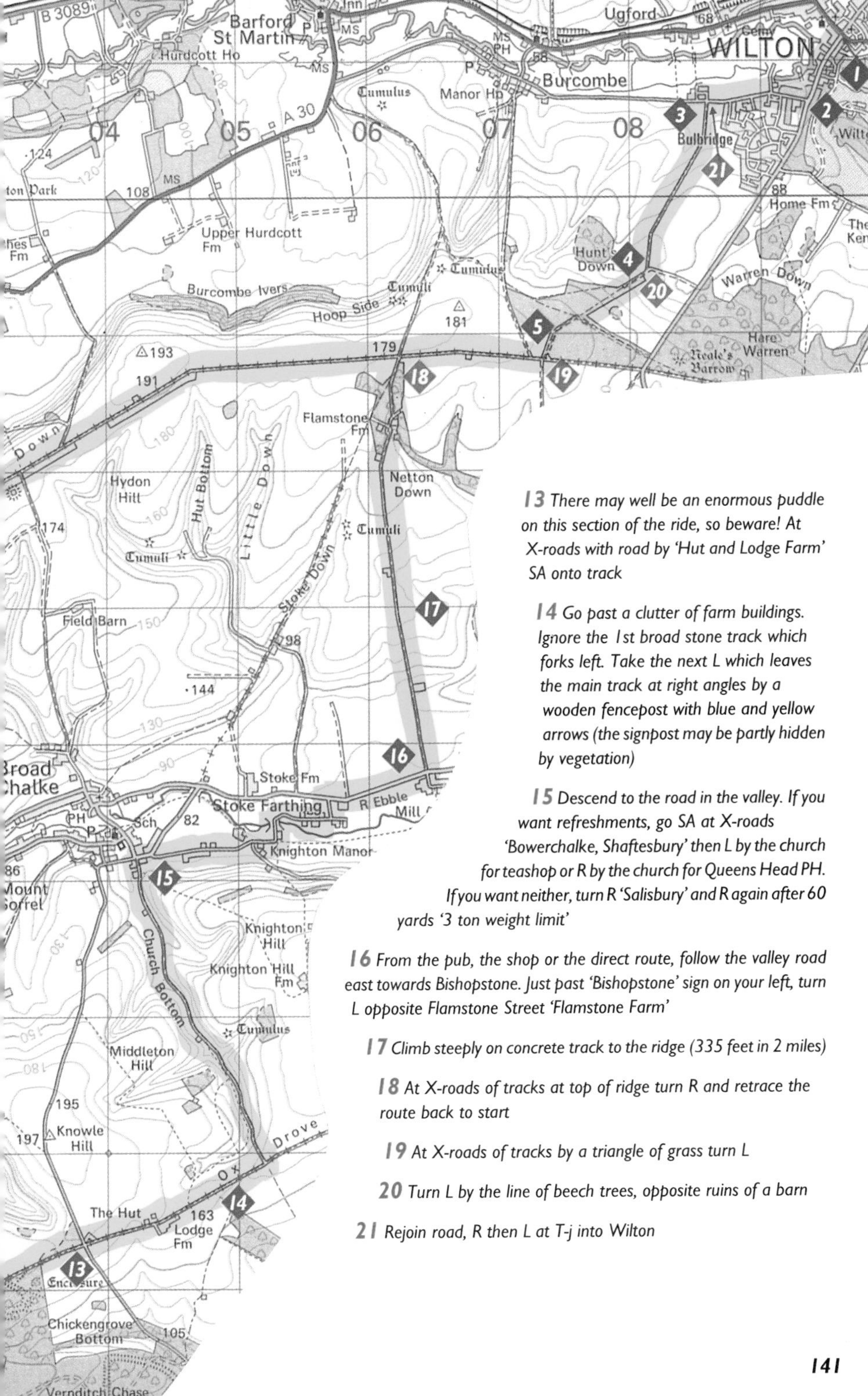

__13__ There may well be an enormous puddle on this section of the ride, so beware! At X-roads with road by 'Hut and Lodge Farm' SA onto track

__14__ Go past a clutter of farm buildings. Ignore the 1st broad stone track which forks left. Take the next L which leaves the main track at right angles by a wooden fencepost with blue and yellow arrows (the signpost may be partly hidden by vegetation)

__15__ Descend to the road in the valley. If you want refreshments, go SA at X-roads 'Bowerchalke, Shaftesbury' then L by the church for teashop or R by the church for Queens Head PH. If you want neither, turn R 'Salisbury' and R again after 60 yards '3 ton weight limit'

__16__ From the pub, the shop or the direct route, follow the valley road east towards Bishopstone. Just past 'Bishopstone' sign on your left, turn L opposite Flamstone Street 'Flamstone Farm'

__17__ Climb steeply on concrete track to the ridge (335 feet in 2 miles)

__18__ At X-roads of tracks at top of ridge turn R and retrace the route back to start

__19__ At X-roads of tracks by a triangle of grass turn L

__20__ Turn L by the line of beech trees, opposite ruins of a barn

__21__ Rejoin road, R then L at T-j into Wilton